Summer Quest!™

Summer Workbook Series

Note: All activities with young children should be performed with adult supervision. Caregivers should be aware of allergies, sensitivities, health, and safety issues.

Credit

Production: Shakespeare Squared LLC

Rainbow Bridge
An imprint of Carson-Dellosa Publishing LLC
P.O. Box 35665
Greensboro, NC 27425 USA

ISBN 978-1-60095-385-9

Table of Contents

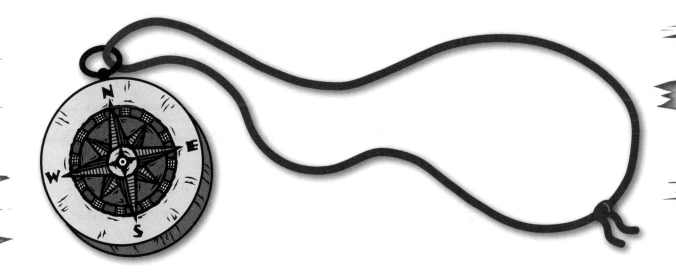

Encouraging Summer Reading

Literacy is the single most important skill that your child needs to be successful in school. The following list includes ideas of ways that you can help your child discover the great adventures of reading!

- Establish a time for reading each day. Ask your child about what he or she is reading. Try to relate the material to an event that is happening this summer or to another book or story.

- Let your child see you reading for enjoyment. Talk about the great things that you discover when you read.

- Create a summer reading list. Choose books from the reading list (pages v–vi) or head to the library and explore the shelves. A general rule for selecting books at the appropriate reading level is to choose a page and ask your child to read it aloud. If he or she does not know more than five words on the page, the book may be too difficult.

- Read newspaper and magazine articles, recipes, menus, maps, and street signs on a daily basis to show your child the importance of reading.

- Find books that relate to your child's experiences. For example, if you are going camping, find a book about camping. This will help your child develop new interests.

- Visit the library each week. Let your child choose his or her own books, but do not hesitate to ask your librarian for suggestions. Often, librarians can recommend books based on what your child enjoyed in the past.

- Make up stories. This is especially fun to do in the car, on camping trips, or while waiting at the airport. Encourage your child to tell a story with a beginning, a middle, and an end. Or, have your child start a story and let other family members build on it.

- Encourage your child to join a summer reading club at the library or a local bookstore. Your child may enjoy talking to other children about the books that he or she has read.

Summer Reading List

The summer reading list includes fiction and nonfiction titles. Experts recommend that parents read with first- and second-grade children for at least 15 minutes each day. Then, ask questions about the story to reinforce comprehension.

Branley, Franklyn M.
The Big Dipper
Gravity Is a Mystery
What Makes Day and Night

Cannon, Janell
Stellaluna

Cooney, Barbara
Miss Rumphius

Cummings, Pat
Clean Your Room, Harvey Moon!

dePaola, Tomie
Jamie O'Rourke and the Big Potato
Strega Nona

DK Publishing
Eye Wonder: Bugs
Eye Wonder: Reptiles

Eastman, P. D.
Are You My Mother?

Fox, Mem
Wilfrid Gordon McDonald Partridge

Gannett, Ruth Stiles
My Father's Dragon

Gove, Doris
My Mother Talks to Trees

Heiligman, Deborah
Jump into Science: Honeybees

Hesse, Karen
Come On, Rain!

Hoban, Russell
A Bargain for Frances

Hoffman, Mary
Amazing Grace

Hoose, Phillip M.
Hey, Little Ant

James, Simon
The Birdwatchers
Dear Mr. Blueberry

Kellogg, Steven
Best Friends

Krudop, Walter Lyon
Something Is Growing

Lakin, Patricia
Dad and Me in the Morning

Locker, Thomas
Where the River Begins

Matsuno, Masako
A Pair of Red Clogs

Summer Reading List (continued)

McCloskey, Robert
Blueberries for Sal
Lentil

McGovern, Ann
...If You Sailed on the Mayflower in 1620

McLerran, Alice
Roxaboxen

Munsch, Robert
The Paper Bag Princess

Murawski, Darlyne A.
Bug Faces

Newman, Marjorie
Mole and the Baby Bird

Nolan, Dennis
Dinosaur Dream

Palatini, Margie
Stinky Smelly Feet: A Love Story

Pfeffer, Wendy
Wiggling Worms at Work

Rylant, Cynthia
When I Was Young in the Mountains

Say, Allen
Emma's Rug

Sendak, Maurice
Pierre: A Cautionary Tale in Five Chapters and a Prologue

Seuss, Dr.
Horton Hatches the Egg
How the Grinch Stole Christmas

Showers, Paul
Where Does the Garbage Go?

Steig, William
Doctor De Soto
Sylvester and the Magic Pebble

Stevens, Janet
Tops & Bottoms

Stevenson, James
The Castaway

Talley, Carol
Papa Piccolo

Titus, Eve
Anatole

Zagwÿn, Deborah Turney
Apple Batter

Zoehfeld, Kathleen Weidner
What Is the World Made Of?: All About Solids, Liquids, and Gases

Skills Checklist

With this book, your child will have the opportunity to practice and acquire many new skills. Keep track of the skills you practice together. Put a check beside each skill your child completes.

Math

- [ ] addition
- [ ] calendar skills
- [ ] fact families
- [ ] fractions
- [ ] geometry
- [ ] graphs and grids
- [ ] measurement
- [ ] multiplication
- [ ] numbers
- [ ] patterns
- [ ] place value
- [ ] reading and writing numbers
- [ ] story problems
- [ ] subtraction
- [ ] symmetry
- [ ] time and money

Language Arts

- [ ] alphabetizing
- [ ] dictionary skills
- [ ] fact and opinion
- [ ] grammar
- [ ] handwriting
- [ ] parts of speech
- [ ] phonics
- [ ] placing events in sequence
- [ ] punctuation
- [ ] puzzles and riddles
- [ ] reading poetry
- [ ] reading stories
- [ ] rhyming
- [ ] sentence structure
- [ ] spelling and proofreading
- [ ] vocabulary
- [ ] word parts
- [ ] writing

Skills Checklist (continued)

Physical Fitness/Health

☐ fitness activities   ☐ outdoor activities

☐ movement   ☐ games

☐ stretching

Social Studies

☐ character development   ☐ map skills

☐ communities   ☐ research skills

☐ geography

Science

☐ climate   ☐ geology

☐ experiment

▶ **Say the name of each picture. Circle the letter of each beginning sound.**

1.

b   g

2.

l   n

3.

b   l

▶ **Say the name of each picture. Circle the letter of each ending sound.**

4.

p   r

5.

t   h

6.

j   r

You can use things you find outside to draw! Find several brightly colored things, like grass, leaves, and flower petals. Rub them on a white piece of paper to see the colors they leave behind. Can you use your natural objects to make a picture?

1

► **Write the capital letters of the alphabet.**

A B

Choose a letter from your name. Now, see how many objects you can find that start with that letter. Write them down. Try to find at least ten different objects.

▶ **Say the name of each picture. Write the vowel that completes each word.**

1.

   m____p

2.

   c____t

3.

   b____d

4.

   c____p

5.

   p____n

6.

   t____p

Fold a piece of paper in half and in half again so that when you unfold it, you have four sections. Now, go outside. Draw something that you see in the first section, something that you hear in the second section, something that you smell in the third section, and something that you can feel in the fourth section.

▶ **Solve each problem.**

1. 5 − 1	**2.** 6 − 4	**3.** 3 − 2
4. 5 + 3	**5.** 9 − 3	**6.** 8 + 2
7. 3 + 3	**8.** 7 − 1	**9.** 8 − 4
10. 6 + 2	**11.** 7 − 4	**12.** 4 + 3

Sunlight and water can make a rainbow. Try making a rainbow with a hose on a sunny day. Turn the water on so that it does not come out too fast. Now, put your thumb over the nozzle hole so that the water sprays out in a mist. Can you see a rainbow?

▶ **Say the name of each picture. Circle the letter of each beginning sound.**

1.

v   n

2.

b   x

3.

f   n

▶ **Say the name of each picture. Circle the letter of each ending sound.**

4.

n   t

5.

m   g

6.

k   y

Find ten small objects. Put them in order by size. Then, try putting them into alphabetical order.

5

▶ **Write the lowercase letters of the alphabet.**

a b

Did you know that a banana has three sections? Peel a banana. Then, push your finger into the top of the banana. The banana should split into three long sections. Do not forget to eat your banana sections!

▶ **Say the name of each picture. Write the letters of the beginning and ending sounds.**

1.

   ____ e ____

2.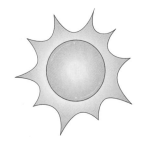

   ____ u ____

3.

   ____ a ____

4.

   ____ e ____

5.

   ____ i ____

6.

   ____ a ____

Around noon, have a friend or family member trace your shadow on the pavement with chalk. Stand in the same place a few hours later and compare your shadow to the outline. How did it change?

7

► **Write the correct time for each clock that has hands. Draw hands on each clock that has a time below it.**

1.

9:00

2.

4:00

3.

___:___

4.

8:00

5.

___:___

6.

11:00

Next time you are in a crowded place, try playing the "ing" game with a friend or family member. To play, take turns finding as many "ing" words as you can to describe what you see happening around you. For example, you might see laughing, swinging, and carrying.

8

▶ **Say the name of each picture. Write the letter of each long vowel sound.**

1.

   _____

2.

   _____

3.

   _____

4.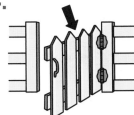

   _____

5.

   _____

6.

   _____

You can bend water! Rub a plastic comb on your hair for about ten seconds. Then, turn on the water in the sink. Adjust the faucet so it makes a small, steady stream. Hold the comb close to (but not in!) the stream of water and see what happens.

9

▶ **Count the dots above each line. Print the correct number word.**

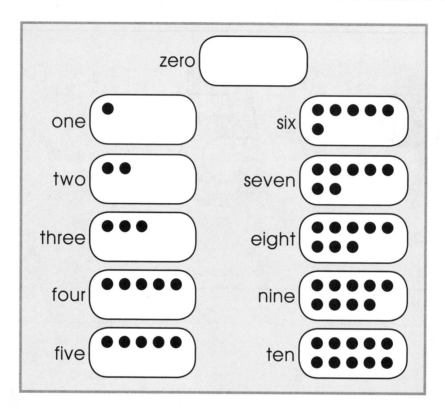

zero [   ]

one [•]   six [••••• •]

two [••]   seven [•••• ••]

three [•••]   eight [••• •••]

four [••••]   nine [••• ••• •••]

five [•••••]   ten [••••• •••••]

1. •

2. ••••• •

3. •••

_____   _____   _____

4.

5. •••••

6. ••••• •••••

_____   _____   _____

How many different kinds of leaves can you find? Go on a leaf hunt. Try to group your leaves by size or shape.

▶ **Say the name of each picture. Circle the word that names each picture.**

1.

tap   tape

2.

mop   mope

3.

slid   slide

4.

cap   cape

You can make a frozen treat with a paper cup and a plastic spoon. Just pour your favorite kind of juice into a small paper cup. Add a plastic spoon for a handle (do not worry if the spoon leans to one side). Put your cup in the freezer overnight. The next day, you can peel the paper cup away and eat your yummy treat!

11

▶ **Complete each number pattern.**

1. 1, 2, _____ , _____ , 5, 6, _____ , _____ , 9, 10, _____ , _____ , 13,

   14, _____ , _____ , 17, 18, _____ , _____ , 21, 22, _____ , _____

2. 31, _____ , _____ , 34, _____ , _____ , 37, _____ , _____ , 40, _____ ,

   _____ , 43, _____ , _____ , 46, _____ , _____ , 49, _____

3. _____ , _____ , 77, 78, _____ , _____ , _____ , 82, _____ , _____ , 85,

   _____ , _____ , _____ , 89, _____ , _____ , 92, _____ , _____ , 95,

   _____ , _____ , 98, _____ , _____ , _____

It can be fun to watch small wild animals like squirrels, rabbits, and birds. Go on a backyard animal quest. How many different animals do you see? Remember to always stay at least ten feet away from wild animals, and never touch them!

▶ **Say the name of each picture. Circle the word that names each picture.**

1.

   can   cane

2.

   pan   pane

3.

   pin   pine

4.

   cub   cube

 Make a paperclip move without touching it. Use one hand to hold an index card. Put a paperclip on top of the card. With your other hand, press a magnet to the underside of the card. Can you make the paperclip move by moving the magnet?

13

▶ **Practice writing your first and last names.**

Find ten quarters (ask an adult if you can borrow some of his or hers). Put them in order by date starting with the oldest quarter. Then, put them in ABC order using the names of the states. Finally, put them in order by how much you like the pictures.

► **Write the correct punctuation mark at the end of each sentence. Use ., !, or ?.**

1. Do you like carrots _____

2. Jan can blow bubbles _____

3. Can you jump rope _____

4. That movie was great _____

5. The woman is happy _____

6. Are bears fuzzy _____

7. Babies drink milk _____

8. Are clouds white _____

9. Watch out for that puddle _____

10. What is your name _____

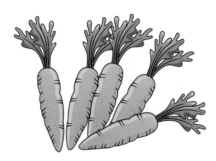

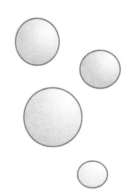

Find a flower or a tree that you like. What do you like about the flower or tree? Write six words that describe it. Use your words to write a poem.

15

► **Count the money for each problem. Write each amount on the lines.**

1¢	**5¢**	**10¢**	**25¢**
penny	nickel	dime	quarter
1¢	5¢	10¢	25¢

1.   1¢ 1¢ 1¢ 1¢   _____ ¢

2. 10¢ 10¢ 1¢ 1¢   _____ ¢

3. 10¢ 10¢ 5¢ 1¢   _____ ¢

4. 10¢ 5¢ 5¢ 5¢   _____ ¢

5. 25¢ 25¢ 10¢ 1¢   _____ ¢

Find the nutrition facts on a box of cereal. Look for the part that tells how many grams of sugar are in a serving of cereal. Which cereal in your house has the least sugar? Which has the most?

▶ **Say the name of each picture. Write the letter of each short vowel sound.**

1.

___

2.

___

3.

___

4.

___

5.

___

6.

___

 You can make a puzzle. Cut a file folder in half at the fold. Color a picture on one of the halves. Cut it into nine or ten odd-shaped pieces. Now, give the pieces to a friend or family member to put back together.

▶ **Continue each pattern.**

Symbols

1. □ △ □ △ □ △ _____ _____ _____ _____ _____

2. ☆ ○ ▭ ☆ ○ ▭ _____ _____ _____ _____ _____

3. ◇ ◇ ⬭ ◇ ◇ ⬭ _____ _____ _____ _____ _____

4. □ ⬆ ⬆ □ ⬆ ⬆ _____ _____ _____ _____ _____

Numbers

5. 1 2 1 2 1 2 _____ _____ _____ _____ _____ _____

6. 5 4 6 5 4 6 5 4 _____ _____ _____ _____ _____

7. 9 9 8 9 9 8 9 9 8 _____ _____ _____ _____ _____

8. 1 5 2 5 1 5 2 5 1 5 2 5 _____ _____ _____ _____

How many different kinds of plants are in your backyard? Take paper, a pencil, and a clipboard outside. Draw a small picture of each different plant you see.

▶ **Read each sentence. Then, draw a picture of your favorite sentence.**

The cat sat on Alfonso's lap.

The cat plays with the ball.

The boy has a pet frog.

The frog hops on Sam's bed.

Ask an adult to help you poke small holes in the bottom of a paper cup with a thumbtack. Tape the open end of the cup over the end of a flashlight. Go into a dark room and shine the flashlight at a wall. Do you see tiny dots of light?

▶ **Circle the words that rhyme with the first word in each row.**

1. cat	hat	wig	bat	man	sat
2. bag	rag	tag	dog	big	sag
3. he	she	me	we	go	see
4. cake	rake	late	lake	make	bake
5. sing	ring	song	thing	wing	big
6. run	fun	gum	sun	spun	tin
7. hand	fan	land	sand	kind	band

What is outside your bedroom window? Without looking, make a list of six things you are likely to see. Then, go look out your window and see if they are all there.

20

▶ **Read the directions. Then, draw the picture.**

Draw a tree.

Draw a bird in the tree.

Draw a flower.

Draw a girl sitting on a rock.

Write a title for the picture on the line.

_____

Put a teaspoon of baking soda on a plate. Pour a few drops of vinegar onto the baking soda. What happens?

▶ **Solve each word problem.**

1. Susan had a nickel. She found another nickel. Her mother gave her two dimes for taking out the trash. How much money does she have now?

_____ ¢

2. Tyrone wants to buy ice cream at lunch. Lunch costs 50¢ and ice cream costs 25¢. If Tyrone has $1.00, does he have enough to buy both?

    Yes   No

3. Maria took 50¢ to the store. She spent 10¢ on candy, 10¢ on popcorn, and 15¢ on a drink. How much money did she spend?

_____ ¢

How much does she have left?

_____ ¢

How many different kinds of vegetables can you list? Write them all down on a piece of paper. Underline all the ones that you have tried. Put a star next to the ones you like best. Put an "X" near the ones you do not like.

▶ **Draw a line to match each word to its opposite.**

1. in   down

2. up   out

3. big   old

4. tall   over

5. new   short

6. under   little

7. soft   stay

8. hot   cold

9. off   hard

10. happy   no

11. go   on

12. yes   sad

Put a squirt of dish soap and a few drops of food coloring into a bowl of warm water. Use a straw to mix it all up. Then, blow through the straw to make bubbles. Put a piece of paper on top of your bubbles to make a bubble print.

23

▶ Follow the directions below to move like a starfish.

Moving around makes you more flexible. Many ocean animals, such as crabs, octopuses, and starfish, move in unique ways. Practice their ways of getting around. Think about a starfish. It moves by using suction on the bottom of each arm. Pretend that you are a starfish by lying on your stomach, spreading your hands and feet on the floor, and looking facedown. Push up on your toes and hands. Pretend that each of your hands and feet is a starfish foot. Move one "foot" at a time and try to move forward. It requires flexibility to keep your body stretched out. Depending on how far you move like a starfish, you can build strength and endurance too.

What did your parents like to do when they were your age? Find out by asking them. Ask your grandparents too.

24

▶ **Solve each word problem.**

1. Grayson's train has 2 green cars and 7 red cars. How many train cars does Grayson's train have in all?

2. Six deer are standing in a field. Two deer run away. How many deer are left in the field?

3. David has 9 spelling words. He misspells 2 words. How many words does he spell correctly?

4. Magdalena has 7 markers. She finds 3 more markers under her bed. How many markers does Magdalena have in all?

Make a necklace out of o-shaped cereal. If the cereal comes in different colors, make a pattern. Then, you can eat your necklace!

25

▶ **Write the contraction from the word bank that means the same thing as each word pair.**

we'll	he's	I'm	she'll
it's	you'll	it'll	they've

1. it is _____

2. they have _____

3. we will _____

4. I am _____

5. you will _____

6. she will _____

7. he has _____

8. it will _____

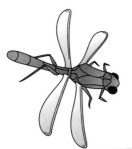  

How many letters are in your whole name? Who has the longest name in your family? Who has the shortest?

► **Count by 2s. Fill in the missing numerals.**

1. 2 _____ 6 _____ _____ 12

2. 14 _____ _____ 20 _____ _____

3. _____ 28 _____ _____ 34 _____

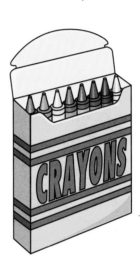

► **Count by 5s. Fill in the missing numerals.**

4. 5 _____ _____ 20 _____ _____

5. 35 _____ 45 _____ _____

6. 65 _____ _____ 80 _____ _____

One way that people are different from other mammals is that we have thumbs. To see how important thumbs are, ask an adult to tape your thumbs to the sides of your hand so that you cannot move them. Now, try to do everyday things such as writing, making your bed, and eating.

▶ **Write each group of words in alphabetical order.**

1. apple _____

   cat _____

   book _____

2. dog _____

   fish _____

   eagle _____

3. girl _____

   ice _____

   hat _____

4. lamp _____

   king _____

   map _____

You can tell if an egg is hardboiled by spinning it. Try spinning two eggs: one that has been hardboiled and one that has not. Why do you think the hardboiled egg spins better than the egg that was not hardboiled?

► **Count the tens and ones. Write each number.**

1.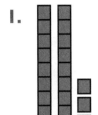

_____

2.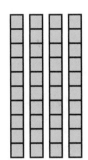

_____

3.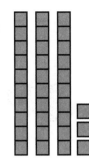

_____

4.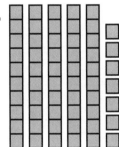

_____

5.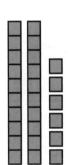

_____

6.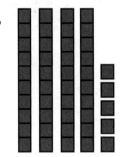

_____

Take a piece of string about as long as your arm and use it to make a circle in the grass. Look very carefully at what is inside your circle. You might want to use a magnifying glass. What do you see?

▶ **Circle the word that names each picture. Then, draw a picture of one of the other words in each list.**

1.

boy

bone

bow

2.

eagle

egg

eye

3.

sun

sand

snake

Make a sand drawing. Use white glue to make a design on a heavy piece of paper or cardboard. Sprinkle dry sand all over the paper. Wait for the glue to dry, and then tip the paper to get rid of the extra sand.

▶ **Count by 10s. Fill in the missing numerals.**

1. 10 _____ _____ 40 _____ 60 _____

2. 30 _____ _____ 60 _____ _____ _____

3. _____ 50 _____ _____ _____ _____ 100

4. 20 _____ _____ 50 _____ _____ _____

5. 10 _____ 30 _____ _____ 60 _____

6. _____ 50 _____ _____ 80 _____ 100

Get four or five glasses that are all the same size. Fill them with different amounts of water. Now, use a spoon to gently tap each of the glasses. Do the glasses sound the same or different?

► **Write the name of the month it is right now. Fill in the calendar with the correct dates for the month.**

Month:

Sunday	Monday	Tuesday	Wednesday	Thursday	Friday	Saturday

1. How many days are in one week? _____

2. How many days are in this month? _____

3. How many months are in a year? _____

Make a list of ten natural things, such as a small rock or a leaf that has been nibbled on by a bug. Challenge a friend or family member to find everything on your list, or find everything yourself.

▶ **Think of three ways to finish this sentence. Write your sentences on the lines.**

I liked first grade because . . .

1. _____

_____.

2. _____

_____.

3. _____

_____.

Make an animal book. Use a notebook or small sketchbook. Draw pictures of the animals you see in nature. You can draw different kinds of birds, insects, fish, and small mammals such as squirrels.

33

▶ **Count the money for each problem. Write each amount on the line.**

1.
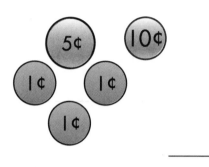
_____¢

2.
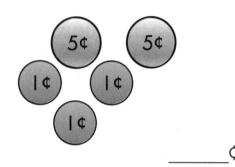
_____¢

3.
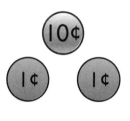
_____¢

4.
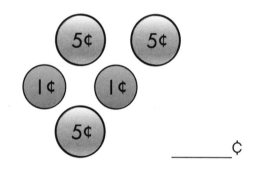
_____¢

5.
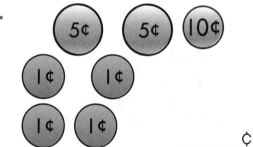
_____¢

6.
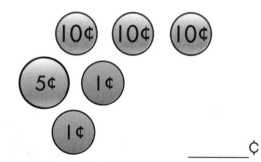
_____¢

How many different light bulbs are in your house? Make a guess and write it down. Then, check your guess by counting all the light bulbs.

34

▶ **Circle the word that completes each sentence. Write the word on the line.**

1. At night, the sky is _____ .

   day   dark   down

2. The _____ came to the party.

   game   sun   girls

3. A rabbit can _____ to the fence.

   hop   hat   boy

4. Andy's dog got _____ in the pond.

   wet   when   hop

Do this activity on a sunny day. Put several small objects on a darkly colored piece of construction paper. Put the paper and the objects in a sunny place. Come back a few hours later and remove the objects. What happened to the paper?

► **Read each sentence. Write the correct noun from the word bank on the line.**

nest	doctor	dentist	teacher
piano	school	pencil	store

1. This is a thing used to make music. _____

2. This person checks your teeth. _____

3. This place sells things you need. _____

4. This is a thing you use to write. _____

5. This person helps you learn at school. _____

6. This place is where children go to learn. _____

7. This is a thing in which a bird lays eggs. _____

8. This person works in a hospital. _____

Find something in nature for every color of the rainbow. Write down the name of each color. Then, write what you found to go with each color.

► **Fill in each blank. Ask an adult if you need help.**

When I was a baby, I learned to talk. I learned to talk when

I was _____ months old. My first words were

_____, _____,

_____, and _____.

If babies could talk even more, they would tell us _____

_____

_____

_____

_____.

Get two paper towels wet with water. Lay one of them out flat to dry in the sun. Crumple the other one up and put it in the sun. Which one do you think will dry first?

37

► **Draw a line to match the price of each toy with the correct amount of money.**

1.  47¢

2.  26¢

3.  38¢

4.  18¢

 Butterflies are attracted to bright colors like red, yellow, purple, and pink. Try wearing a brightly colored hat or shirt. Look for a place where there are butterflies, like a park or garden. If you stand very still, a butterfly may land on you. Remember never to touch a butterfly – the oils from your fingers can hurt the butterfly's wings.

► **Read your favorite story. Describe it by filling in the story web below with words, sentences, or pictures.**

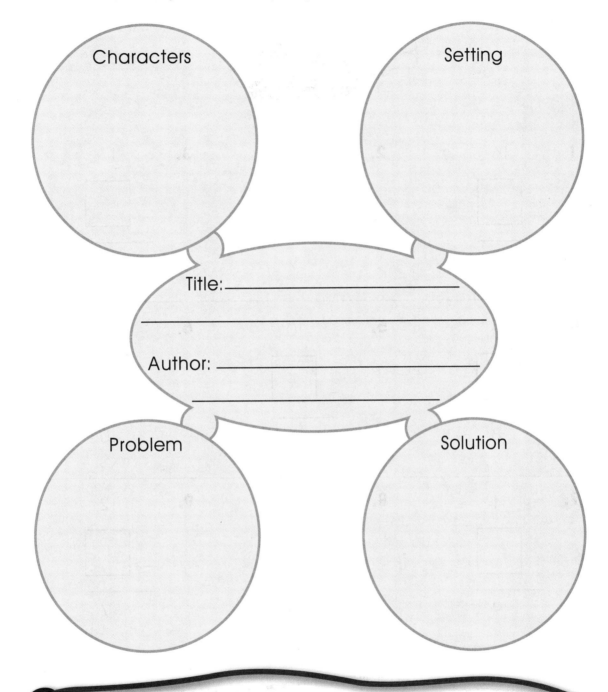

Characters

Setting

Title:_____

_____

Author: _____

_____

Problem

Solution

Trace your hand six or seven times in different positions on a piece of white paper. Your hands should overlap. Color the spaces to make an interesting design.

39

► **Fill in the missing numbers.**

1.
$$16 - \boxed{} = 8$$

2.
$$15 - \boxed{} = 9$$

3.
$$17 - \boxed{} = 8$$

4.
$$14 - \boxed{} = 8$$

5.
$$10 - \boxed{} = 6$$

6.
$$8 - \boxed{} = 0$$

7.
$$11 - \boxed{} = 9$$

8.
$$9 - \boxed{} = 9$$

9.
$$12 - \boxed{} = 7$$

Drop a ball of clay into a bowl of water and watch it sink. See if you can make it float by making it into a shallow bowl shape. Why do you think changing the shape makes the clay float?

► **Capitalize the** *first word in a sentence*, *days of the week*, *months*, **and** *proper names* **of people and places.**

EXAMPLE: We took Rhonda to New York on a Friday in June.

► **Circle the letters that need to be capitalized.**

1. she played ball on our team.

2. dr. sharma is our dentist.

3. do you know paul brown?

4. we are going to atlanta in december.

5. may we go to the park on sunday?

6. on tuesday we can go swimming.

7. are you going with us on wednesday?

8. please call robin stuart tonight.

9. our teacher this year is mr. perry.

Find out what foods ants like best. Put several small pieces of food on a paper plate. You could try cereal flakes, carrot or cheese shavings, sugar, apple bits, or popcorn. Put the plate outside near a place where you have seen ants. Watch to see what the ants take.

► **Measure each object with the ruler shown. Write each object's length in inches.**

1.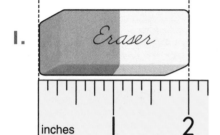

_____ in.

2.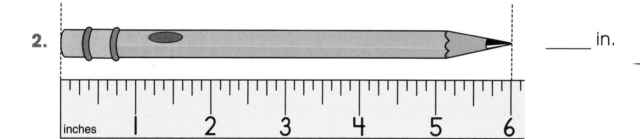

_____ in.

Next time you are at the beach, experiment with your footprints. First, make footprints in the dry sand. Then, make prints where the sand is damp, but not soaking wet. Finally, make prints very close to the water, where the sand is very wet. Where were your prints the clearest?

▶ **Circle the letter of the phrase that tells what each poem is about.**

1. This is a man who is usually wealthy.

   He might live a long time if he keeps himself healthy.

   His castle's his home, but there's one special thing.

   He can always say, "Dad," when he talks to the king.

   A. a king   B. a president

   C. a doctor   D. a prince

2. I have never seen them, but I have heard them scurry.

   When I open the cupboard door, they leave in a hurry.

   They never say, "Please," when they take all of our cheese,

   And they do not like our big, gray cat Murray.

   A. relatives   B. mice

   C. friends   D. cats

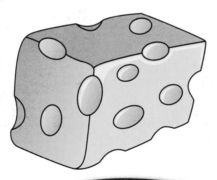

Go on a texture hunt. Use white paper and a dark crayon with the paper peeled off. Put your paper against an interesting texture, like the trunk of a tree or the side of a house. Rub the side of your crayon on the paper to record the texture.

43

▶ **Write the correct punctuation mark at the end of each sentence. Use . or ?.**

1. Do you like puzzles_____

2. We are going to the beach today_____

3. What time do you go to bed_____

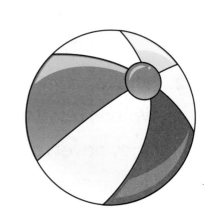

4. Is that frog green_____

5. They will eat dinner later_____

6. It is time to go to bed_____

Find as many green things as you can in nature. Put them in order by starting with the thing that is the darkest shade of green and ending with the lightest shade.

▶ **Solve each problem.**

1. $5 + 6 =$ _____

2. $9 - 5 =$ _____

3. $7 + 3 =$ _____

4. $8 - 3 =$ _____

5. $10 + 1 =$ _____

6. $10 - 4 =$ _____

7. $2 + 9 =$ _____

8. $8 - 2 =$ _____

9. $7 + 4 =$ _____

10. $9 - 3 =$ _____

11. $6 + 5 =$ _____

12. $3 + 8 =$ _____

13. $9 + 3 =$ _____

14. $6 + 4 =$ _____

15. $6 - 4 =$ _____

A walking stick is a good thing to have for walks and hikes. Look around your yard or a park for a sturdy stick about the same size as you are. Ask an adult to remove branches that you do not want. You can decorate your walking stick with bells, pieces of string, or paint.

▶ **Draw a line to match each sentence with the correct job.**

EXAMPLE:

I deliver letters and packages.   farmer

1. I help people get well.   pilot

2. I grow things to eat.   mail carrier

3. I fly airplanes.   teacher

4. I work in a school.   baker

5. I bake cakes and bread.   doctor

Write a three-letter word at the top of a piece of paper. Change one letter to make a new word, and write it under the first word. Change a letter in the second word to make a new word, and write it under the second word. Keep going until you cannot make any new words.

▶ **Read each word. Color the space blue if the word has the long /ī/ sound. Color the space green if the word has the short /ĭ/ sound.**

bib	fry	tie	light	my	sigh	try	wig
six	bike	sign	pie	guy	by	high	if
fib	gift	pit	dry	bite	miss	fish	lit
chin	sit	hill	time	night	hid	bill	quit
bin	mitt	tin	cry	dime	win	fit	will
pin	fine	lie	sight	why	right	shy	fin
zip	ride	buy	side	hike	kite	nine	did

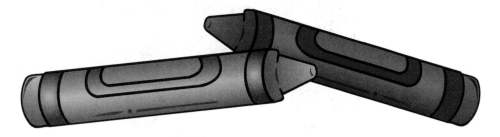

Make your name by cutting out letters from a magazine and gluing them onto a piece of paper. Try to find big letters.

▶ **Underline the misspelled word in each sentence. Spell the word correctly on the line.**

1. Ebony backed a cake. _____

2. Libby and I whent to the zoo. _____

3. William has a trane. _____

4. Clean your rom! _____

5. Where is your bik? _____

Find three things in your room that you no longer use. Give them to a younger brother or sister, or ask an adult to donate them to a charity.

▶ **Read the story. Then, draw how you think the story will end.**

The Sinking Lily Pad

Frog liked to sit on a lily pad in the pond. He loved to catch bugs, too. When he ate too many bugs, the lily pad sank into the water.

▶ **Write a sentence to tell about your picture.**

_____

_____

Find several natural things from your yard, such as leaves, pinecones, stones, and twigs. Lay them out on a porch or on the pavement. Challenge a friend or family member to find a similar object to go with each thing you found.

49

▶ **Complete each fact family.**

1. Family: 2, 3, 5

    2 + 3 = ☐

    3 + ☐ = 5

    5 − 2 = ☐

    ☐ − 3 = 2

2. Family: 2, 7, 9

    7 + 2 = ☐

    ☐ + 7 = 9

    9 − ☐ = 2

    9 − ☐ = 7

3. Family: 3, 5, 8

    5 + 3 = ☐

    ☐ + ☐ = 8

    8 − ☐ = ☐

    ☐ − 3 = ☐

4. Family: 3, 4, 7

    3 + 4 = ☐

    ☐ + ☐ = 7

    7 − ☐ = 3

    ☐ − 3 = 4

Put an uncooked egg in a glass of water and watch it sink to the bottom. Now, take out the egg and add about twelve heaping spoonfuls of salt. Mix the salt into the water. Now, put the egg in the water again. What happened?

▶ **Write the correct color words.**

1. A snowflake is _____.

2. Chocolate is _____.

3. Plums are _____.

4. Blueberries are _____.

5. A frog is _____.

6. A pumpkin is _____.

7. A banana is _____.

8. A tire is _____.

9. Cherries are _____.

10. A pencil eraser is _____.

Roll a pair of dice twenty times. Every time you roll the dice, write down the sum of the two dice on a piece of paper. Which sum came up the most? Why do you think that happened?

51

▶ **Add to find each sum.**

1.	38 + 7	**2.**	25 + 6	**3.**	49 + 9
4.	34 + 6	**5.**	46 + 8	**6.**	55 + 8
7.	29 + 3	**8.**	71 + 9	**9.**	68 + 4
10.	53 + 7	**11.**	39 + 4	**12.**	26 + 5

Find a short poem that you like. Memorize it. Recite it for your family.

▶ **Read the story. Then, answer the question.**

At the Pond

One warm, spring day, some ducklings decided to go to a pond. They wanted to swim.

"Can we go too?" asked the chicks.

"Chicks cannot swim," laughed the ducklings.

"We will run in the tall grass and look for bugs. Please let us go with you," begged the chicks. So, the ducklings and the chicks set off for the pond.

The ducklings swam in the pond. They splashed in the water. The chicks ran in the tall grass. They looked for bugs. The ducklings and the chicks had fun.

After a while, the ducklings and the chicks were tired from playing. They missed their mothers. They missed their nests. It was time to go home.

I. Which sentence tells the main idea of the story?

   A. Ducklings have fun swimming.

   B. Chicks and ducklings hatch from eggs.

   C. The ducklings and the chicks had fun at the pond.

Find a notebook and start a happiness journal. Each day, write about something that makes you happy. You can write just one word or several sentences. Add drawings to your journal.

▶ **Add to find each sum.**

1. 7
    + 5

2. 9
    + 7

3. 7
    + 2

4. 4
    + 2

5. 9
    + 2

6. 3
    + 2

7. 4
    + 3

8. 6
    + 1

9. 8
    + 4

10. 5
    + 4

11. 7
    + 6

12. 9
    + 1

Find a road map of your city. There is probably one in the glove box of your family's car. See if you can find familiar places, like the zoo, a park, or your school. Can you find the neighborhood where you live?

54

▶ In a **blend**, like *sl* in *slide*, two consonants make a sound together. Say the name of each picture. Write the letters for the blend in each word.

1.

__ __ __

2.

__ __ __

3.

__ __ __

4.

__ __ __

5.

__ __ __

6.

__ __ __

How many steps would it take you to get from your bedroom to the kitchen? Make a guess, and then check your guess by counting your steps.

55

▶ **Subtract to find each difference.**

1. 10
    − 6
    ‾‾‾‾

2. 10
    − 8
    ‾‾‾‾

3. 13
    − 9
    ‾‾‾‾

4. 16
    − 7
    ‾‾‾‾

5. 15
    − 9
    ‾‾‾‾

6. 8
    − 3
    ‾‾‾‾

7. 4
    − 2
    ‾‾‾‾

8. 11
    − 2
    ‾‾‾‾

9. 12
    − 7
    ‾‾‾‾

10. 9
    − 5
    ‾‾‾‾

11. 14
    − 6
    ‾‾‾‾

12. 7
    − 3
    ‾‾‾‾

Spend some time watching the clouds. How many different shades of white do you see? How fast do the clouds move across the sky? Do any of the cloud shapes look like something you have seen before?

▶ **Draw a line to match each contraction to its word pair.**

EXAMPLE:

didn't   it is

1. it's   we will

2. we're   did not

3. you've   we are

4. don't   is not

5. we'll   you have

6. isn't   do not

You can lift an ice cube with a piece of string. Put an ice cube on a plate and lay a piece of string across the top of it. Pour salt on the ice cube and wait about fifteen seconds. Then, try to lift the ice cube by grabbing the two string-ends.

57

► **Use the picture below to help you match the animals in each row with the words that show their places in line.**

first   second   third   fourth   fifth

1.

third   first   second   fifth   fourth

2.

fourth   fifth   first   third   second

Find three words in the dictionary that you do not know. Learn the meaning of each word. Then, write a short story using all three of your new words.

▶ **Unscramble each sentence. Write the words in the correct order.**

1. swim like Ducks to.

_____

2. we sandbox Can play in the?

_____

3. nests birds in trees Some make.

_____

4. fun today Are having you?

_____

There are probably many different kinds of birds in your backyard or neighborhood park. Sit outside in a quiet place for about fifteen minutes and look for different birds. Put a tally mark on a piece of paper for every different kind of bird you see.

59

▶ Measure each object with the ruler shown. Write each object's length in centimeters.

1. 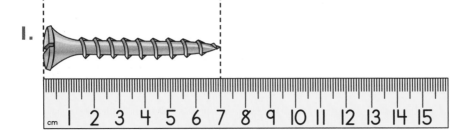 _____ cm

2. _____ cm

 Many kinds of insects and other small animals nibble on leaves. See if you can find a leaf that has been nibbled on by an animal.

▶ **Say the name of each picture. Circle the pictures that have the long /ā/ sound, as in *tape*.**

cake

hand

whale

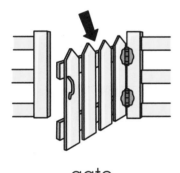

gate

grapes

lamp

You can make your paintings sparkle with salt! Make a picture using watercolor paints. Sprinkle some table salt on your painting while it is still wet. When your picture dries, it will sparkle!

Each word and picture make a compound word. Write each compound word on the line.

1. cook +  = _____

2. base +  = _____

3. butter +  = _____

4.  + fighter = _____

Put ten small objects in a paper bag. Reach your hand inside and see if you can tell what one of the objects is just by touching it. After you have guessed, pull the object out of the bag to see if you were correct. Try all ten objects.

▶ **Read the word on each balloon. Color the balloon red if the word has the long /ū/ sound. Color the balloon blue if the word has the short /ū/ sound.**

1.
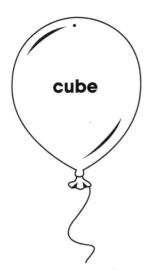
cube

2.

rub

3.
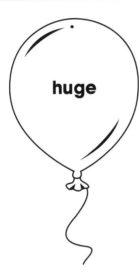
huge

4.

gum

Walk around your house with a magnet. With an adult, use the magnet to see which things are magnetic and which things are not. Fold a piece of paper in half. Draw the things that are magnetic on one side of the fold. Draw the things that are not magnetic on the other side.

63

▶ **Complete each fact family.**

1. Family: 4, 5, 9

$4 + 5 =$ ☐

$5 + 4 =$ ☐

$9 - 5 =$ ☐

$9 - 4 =$ ☐

2. Family: 6, 2, 8

$6 +$ ☐ $= 8$

$2 +$ ☐ $=$ ☐

$8 -$ ☐ $= 2$

$8 -$ ☐ $=$ ☐

3. Family: 3, 7, 10

☐ $+$ ☐ $=$ ☐

☐ $+$ ☐ $=$ ☐

☐ $-$ ☐ $=$ ☐

☐ $-$ ☐ $=$ ☐

4. Family: 1, 8, 9

☐ $+$ ☐ $=$ ☐

☐ $+$ ☐ $=$ ☐

☐ $-$ ☐ $=$ ☐

☐ $-$ ☐ $=$ ☐

Find leaves from two different plants. Look at them carefully. See if you can find three ways that they are different and three ways that they are the same.

▶ **Read the _ir_ words in the word bank. Use them to answer the questions.**

bird	first	girl	twirl	third	circle

1. What is the opposite of boy? _____

2. What grade comes after second? _____

3. What do you do with a baton? _____

4. What's another word for "number one"? _____

5. What animal builds its nest in a tree? _____

6. What shape is round like a ball? _____

Find a good luck charm. A good luck charm can be any small object — a rock, a shell, a penny, or whatever else you can find. Put your new good luck charm in your pocket and carry it with you wherever you go.

▶ **The underlined words tell *who*, *what*, *when*, or *where*. Write the correct word at the beginning of each sentence.**

EXAMPLE:

_____who_____   <u>My mother</u> is going home.

1. _____   We will go swimming <u>tomorrow morning</u>.

2. _____   <u>Devon</u> likes to eat peaches.

3. _____   The book is <u>under the bed</u>.

4. _____   On Sunday, we will go on a <u>picnic</u>.

5. _____   The big truck was stuck <u>in the mud</u>.

6. _____   <u>Monday</u> was the first day of school.

Get 24 pennies and an empty egg carton. If you put the same number of pennies into four of the compartments, how many pennies will go in each one? Try it and see. Then try putting an equal number of pennies in six compartments, then eight compartments, and then all twelve.

▶ **Solve each word problem.**

1. Iman has 3 baseballs. He finds 3 more. How many baseballs does he have in all?

2. A farmer has 9 apples. He makes a pie with 5 of them. How many apples does he have left?

Go outside and see if you can find exactly 100 of the same natural object. For example, you might find 100 pinecones, 100 small rocks, or 100 acorns. Count your natural objects by putting them into groups of ten.

67

► **What does it mean to respect someone? It means to think about someone else's feelings and to show the person that you care. List the names of the three people whom you respect most and tell why. Then, write how you can show them respect. At the top of your list, write** *Respect Really Rules!*

_____

_____

_____

_____

_____

_____

_____

_____

_____

Some animals blend into their environment so they will not be seen by other animals. If you lived in your backyard, what clothing would help you to blend into your environment? Pick out clothes that would help you to blend in, and wear them outside.

▶ **Read the story. Then, answer the question.**

A Place for Little Frog

Little Frog hopped out of the pond. "Where are you going, Little Frog?" asked the other frogs.

"I am tired of living in this pond with so many frogs," he said. "I need more space." So, Little Frog hopped away.

Soon, he met a bee. When he told the bee his story, the bee buzzed, "You cannot live with me. You would get stuck in my honey."

Little Frog said, "Don't worry, bee, your hive is not the place for me."

Next, Little Frog met a dog. The dog barked and chased Little Frog away. "Living with a dog is not the place for me," said Little Frog.

Little Frog hopped and hopped all the way back to his pond. The other frogs were happy to see him. They moved over to make room for him. Little Frog settled in, smiled, and said, "Now, this is the place for me."

I. Which sentence tells the main idea of the story?

A. A hive is no place for a frog.

B. Dogs do not like frogs.

C. Little Frog found out that his own home is best.

Most birds have two kinds of feathers. The ones used for flying are longer and firmer. The ones used to keep the bird warm are smaller, softer, and fluffier. See if you can find one of each kind of feather. You may want to use a magnifying glass to get a closer look at the feathers you find.

► **Write a number sentence for each story problem.**

1. Trevor invited 5 boys to his birthday party.
   He also invited 4 girls.
   How many children did he invite in all?

   _____ + _____ = _____

2. Rachel had 3 bracelets.
   Her mother gave her 1 more bracelet.
   What was the total number of bracelets Rachel had?

   _____ + _____ = _____

3. Jamal's bank had 8 dimes in it.
   Jamal added 2 more dimes.
   Add to find out how many dimes are now in the bank.

   _____ + _____ = _____

Make your own bubble wand. Just cut out the center of a plastic lid from a yogurt or margarine container so that the rim makes an "O" shape. Then, glue the lid-ring to a wooden craft stick. You can make bubble solution by gently mixing a little bit of liquid dish soap with water in a bowl.

▶ **Draw the next object in each pattern.**

1.

2. ▲ ■ ▲ ■ ___

3. ⬭⬭⬭ ★ ⬭⬭⬭ ★ ___

4. ⬠ ● ● ⬠ ● ● ___

How does the world change when the sun sets? Sit in a quiet place just before it begins to get dark. Look for changes with your eyes. Listen for changes with your ears. Write down everything you see and hear.

▶ **Read each riddle. Write a word that rhymes with the underlined word.**

1. It rhymes with <u>hat</u>.

   It is a good pet.

   It is a _____ .

---

2. It rhymes with <u>noise</u>.

   Kids like to play with them.

   They are _____ .

Colors come in many different shades. Write the name of a color at the top of a piece of paper. Then, walk through the rooms in your house. Every time you see a different shade of that color, make a tally mark on your paper. Do the same thing with another color, and compare the results.

► **Fill in the circle beside the sentence that best describes each picture.**

I.

○ The bee is on the flower.

○ The bee is under the flower.

○ The bee is in the hive.

2.

○ The bird is on the bowl.

○ The bird loves to sing.

○ The bird never sings.

Make a bagel bird feeder. First, tie a piece of string through the hole in a bagel. Then, spread peanut butter all over the bagel, and dip it in birdseed, dry oatmeal, or popped popcorn. Hang the feeder from a tree.

73

► **Say the name of each picture. Write _1_ if the word has one syllable. Write _2_ if the word has two syllables.**

1.

   _____

2.

   _____

3.

   _____

4.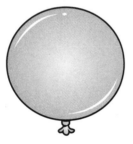

   _____

 Some kinds of black sand are magnetic. Put a magnet in a clear plastic sandwich bag. Drag the baggie with the magnet inside through some sand. The sand that sticks to the baggie is magnetic!

▶ **Complete each number pattern.**

1. 10, 20, _____ , 40, _____ , _____ , 70, _____ , _____ , 100

2. 5, 10, 15, _____ , _____ , _____ , 35, 40, _____ , _____ , 55, _____ ,

_____ , 70, _____ , _____ , _____ , 90, _____ , _____

3. 2, 4, _____ , 8, _____ , 12, _____ , _____ , 18, _____ , 22, _____ , 26,

_____ , _____ , 32, _____ , _____ , _____ , _____ , 42, _____

Put an ice cube in each of two small bowls. Bring the bowls outside into the sun. Put a black piece of paper over the top of one bowl and a white piece of paper over the top of the other bowl. Check your bowls every few minutes. Which ice cube melted faster?

▶ **Say the name of each picture. Write the letter of each vowel sound.**

1.

c____ke

2.

b____x

3.

d____ck

4.

l____mp

5.

m____lk

6.

m____ce

Choose your ten favorite books from your bookshelf. First, put them in order by how many pages each book has. Then, put them in order by the size of the book. Finally, put them in order starting with the one that you like best.

76

▶ **Write the word or phrase that tells where each shape is. The shapes are *on top of*, *under*, or *next to* other shapes.**

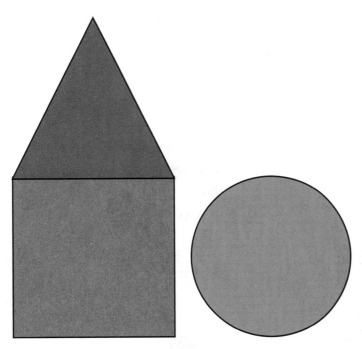

1. The triangle is _____ the square.

2. The circle is _____ the square.

3. The square is _____ the triangle.

Write a letter to a grandparent or other relative. Tell your relative about three different things you have done over the last week. Include a picture.

77

▶ **Draw a line to match each butterfly to the flower with the same long vowel sound.**

beat

peach

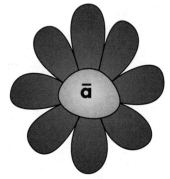

ā

break

leaf

ē

great

steak

Use small yogurt cups to make shakers. Put a small amount of different small objects, such as unpopped popcorn, dried beans, rice, pebbles, sand, paperclips, beads, or seeds into each cup. Put the lids onto the cups. Then, ask a friend or family member to shake the cups and try to guess what is inside.

▶ **Write how many tens and ones are in each number.**

EXAMPLE:

26 = ___2___ tens ___6___ ones

1. 41 = _____ tens _____ one

2. 45 = _____ tens _____ ones

3. 84 = _____ tens _____ ones

4. 65 = _____ tens _____ ones

5. 72 = _____ tens _____ ones

6. 17 = _____ ten _____ ones

7. 39 = _____ tens _____ ones

8. 50 = _____ tens _____ ones

Take a closer look at sand. Put a small amount of sand on a piece of paper – dark colors like black work best, but you can use white, too. Spread out the sand so you can see one grain at a time. Look at your sand with a magnifying glass. Does sand from different places look different?

79

▶ **Draw a line to match each pair of rhyming words.**

EXAMPLE:

goat   tree

1. last   band

2. bee   boat

3. sand   fast

4. blue   hair

5. chair   glue

6. mean   rain

7. main   bean

Make your own mini-golf course. Use boxes, coffee cans, and blocks to create ramps, obstacles, and holes. You can make a golf club by taping a dry sponge to the end of a yardstick.

▶ Number the sentences in the order that the events happened.

1. _____ The sun came out. It became a pretty day.

2. _____ It started to rain.

3. _____ Hannah put her umbrella away.

4. _____ Hannah used her umbrella.

5. _____ The clouds came, and the sky was dark.

Homophones are words that sound the same but are spelled differently, like *meat* and *meet* or *sea* and *see*. Make a list of ten homophone pairs.

▶ **What do you think the perfect tree house would look like? Describe it and draw a picture of it.**

_____

_____

_____

_____

_____

Try to balance a small potato on your finger tip. Gently poke two forks into the potato, one on each side so the ends of the forks are facing down. Can you balance the potato now?

► **Write > or < to compare each set of numbers.**

1. 11 ◯ 13

2. 91 ◯ 87

3. 55 ◯ 75

4. 46 ◯ 29

5. 39 ◯ 27

6. 78 ◯ 33

7. 24 ◯ 19

8. 73 ◯ 85

9. 48 ◯ 100

10. 14 ◯ 21

11. 62 ◯ 56

12. 94 ◯ 78

Different kinds of spiders make different kinds of webs. See if you can find at least two different kinds of webs. Remember not to touch any of the webs you find or the spiders that live in them.

► **Color each pair of synonyms the same color.**

end

little

small

glad

hear

under

happy

listen

below

finish

You will need a table tennis ball and a hair dryer for this activity. Have an adult help you adjust the hair dryer so it blows cool air, and hold it so the air is blowing straight up. Put the table tennis ball in the air stream and see what happens. Can you make it float? What happens if you move the hair dryer?

► **Solve each riddle.**

1. I am tiny. I have three body parts and six legs. I can be a real

    pest at picnics. I am an _____ .

2. I was just born. My mom and dad feed me. I cry and sleep, but I

    cannot walk. I am a _____ .

3. I am made of metal and can be small. I can lock doors and

    unlock them too. I am a _____ .

4. I have four legs. I like to play. I bark. I am a _____ .

Ask a family member for an old sock that is no longer needed. Put the sock over your shoe. Go outside and walk through tall grass or bushes. Take the sock off and shake it over a piece of paper to see if you collected any seeds. How many different kinds of seeds did you get?

▶ Follow the directions below to become more flexible.

Become flexible by pretending that you are rock climbing. Lie on your back and stretch your right arm out in front of you as far as you can. Now, stretch your left leg out in front of you toward the sky. Stretch it as far as it will go. Switch arms and legs. Repeat 10 times. Move slowly as you climb the "mountain."

Fill a bowl with water. Sprinkle some pepper on top of the water. Squirt a few drops of liquid dish soap into the water and see what happens.

86

▶ **Write the correct time for each clock that has hands. Draw hands on each clock that has a time below it.**

1.

2:30

2.

____:____

3.

10:30

4.

____:____

5.

5:00

6.

____:____

You already know that turning off things that use electricity saves energy. Go on an energy hunt. Walk around your house and turn off lights, radios, TVs, and other electrical devices that are not being used. Ask an adult before turning off computers.

87

► **A title tells what a story is about. Write the letter of the title next to the story it matches.**

TITLES		
A. The Turtle Dream	B. The Sleepover	C. A Wish Before Bed

1. _____ Jenna made a wish every night before going to sleep. She would look in the sky for the brightest star. Then, she would close her eyes and make a wish.

2. _____ Malia fell asleep in the car on the way to the beach. She dreamed that she was a flying turtle. She flew all around the beach. No one could catch her.

3. _____ Kendra had her friend Leslie sleep over. They watched a movie and ate popcorn. They made a tent out of blankets. They slept in the tent.

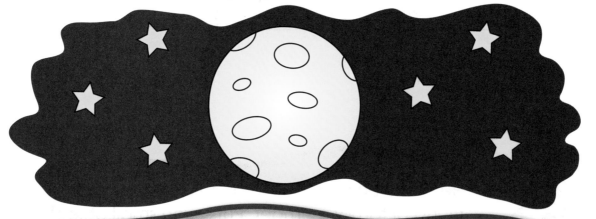

How big is your head? Take a piece of string or yarn and wrap it one time around your head at about the level of your eyes. Ask an adult to cut the string where the two ends meet. Then, use a ruler or yardstick to measure it.

▶ Can you turn a cup of water upside down without spilling it?

Materials:
- index card
- clear plastic cup
- water

Procedure:
1. Do this experiment over a sink.
2. Fill the cup halfway with water.
3. Put the index card on top of the cup. Put your hand over the card. Turn the cup upside down over the sink.
4. Wait two seconds. Then, move your hand away.

What Is This All About?

When you flip the cup, the air outside of the cup pushes on the card. The air pushes harder than the water inside the cup. If you wiggle the card before you move your hand, the water molecules on the card and the rim of the cup will stick together. Then, air cannot get in and equalize the pressure.

Choose an object that you can see right now. If you were to write the name of that object, what would the last letter be? Now find an object that starts with that letter. Keep going as long as you can.

▶ An adjective is a word used to describe a noun.

EXAMPLE: the **green** balloon

▶ Circle the adjectives.

1. the big shoe

2. a tiny pebble

3. the loud radio

4. the colorful dress

5. the yellow bananas

6. a fuzzy puppy

7. the three elephants

8. the chewy taffy

9. a sour lemon

10. the two cupcakes

You can make a kazoo with a cardboard toilet paper roll. Just cut a circle of waxed paper a little bigger than the hole. Cover the hole with the waxed paper circle, and use a rubber band to make it stay. Talk or sing into the other end of your kazoo to make it work.

▶ How do planes fly?

Materials:

- sheet of paper

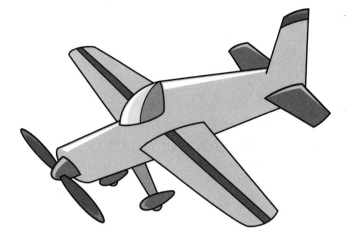

Procedure:

1. Hold a sheet of paper just under your bottom lip. Curve the top of the paper slightly. What do you think will happen to the paper if you blow down and across the top of it? Do you think it will hit you in the chest, stay where it is, or bounce up and hit you in the nose?

2. Write your prediction on a separate sheet of paper.

3. Blow down and across the top of the paper.

What Is This All About?

By blowing down and across the top of the paper, you cause air molecules to move faster across the paper rather than moving around as they normally do. Faster moving air molecules lower the air pressure on the top of the paper. Higher air pressure under the paper pushes the paper up. For an airplane to fly, the air pressure must be lower on top of the wings than under them. The higher air pressure under the wings pushes the airplane up.

Many words go together in pairs, such as *bread* and *butter*, *cat* and *dog*, and *peas* and *carrots*. Make a list of more word pairs. Can you think of at least ten pairs?

▶ Follow the directions below to learn how maps work.

Maps have many uses. A pilot uses maps to find the right flight paths. A hiker uses a map to find her way on a trail. A traveler uses a map to get around a new town.

Work on your mapmaking skills by drawing a map of a path that is in or around your home. You will need a sheet of paper and a pencil. Be as accurate as possible. If you are drawing a path from your room to the refrigerator, include hallways, stairways, rooms, and furniture that you pass as you walk.

Try your map when it is finished. Follow the path as you drew it. Make changes if needed. Then, have a friend or family member try your map. Ask him or her to use the map to follow the path to the end. Have a surprise treat waiting for him or her, such as a snack to share.

Make an alphabet collage. Use old magazines to find a picture for each letter of the alphabet. Cut out your pictures and glue them to a piece of cardboard or poster board. Do not put them in order. See if a friend or family member can find the right picture for each letter.

Write the numbers to complete the hundred chart.

1			4		6	7			
	12			15			18		
21			24		26				30
	33					37		39	
	42				46		48		
51			54			57			60
		63		65				69	
71			74		76				80
		83					88		
91			94			97			100

Everyone knows the poem that starts off, "Roses are red…." Change the second line to, "Lilies are white" and finish the poem. Remember that the last line needs to rhyme with "white."

▶ **Follow the directions below to learn about where you live.**

It is important to learn about where you live. Your state or province might be the home of the first candy factory or the only state or province with a professional trampoline team. With an adult, search the Internet to find interesting information about where you live. Share the fun facts with family and friends. Below are two Web sites to start you on your search.

The Internet Public Library
www.ipl.org/div/stateknow

The World Almanac for Kids
www.worldalmanacforkids.com

Go on a teeny-tiny hunt. Find ten very small objects. Put them in order by size.

▶ Underline the correct plural word.

1.

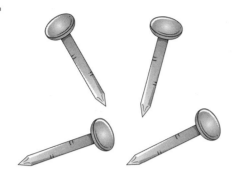

We had to buy (nails, nailes) at the store.

2.

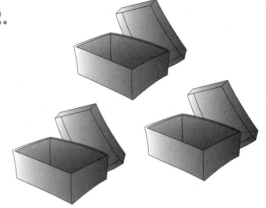

Put the (boxs, boxes) in the garage.

3.

The (dishs, dishes) in the sink are dirty.

4.

We got new (dresss, dresses) today.

Use fresh peas and toothpicks to make a sculpture. Poke the toothpicks into the peas to connect them together. If you let the peas dry, the sculpture will become more solid.

97

▶ **Follow the directions below to pretend you are in another country.**

You can learn a lot about other countries by making and eating some of their native dishes. Think of a country you would like to know more about. Find out what foods the people from that country eat. For example, if you want to learn about France, go to the library with an adult and check out French cookbooks or books about French food. Or, search the Internet with an adult to find recipes for French dishes.

Choose a simple recipe with ingredients that you and an adult can buy at your local grocery store. Whether you make soup, salad, or another treat from the country, you will "taste" a bit of the country when you eat the food. Get your family involved. Invite each family member to choose a country and enjoy trying different foods from places around the world.

Make a list of ten places you would like to visit. They can be close to your home or on the other side of the world. Put a star next to the one you want to visit the most.

▶ **Follow the directions below to get to know nature better.**

In many places, the weather is beautiful outside during the summer. The sun shines. Bright flowers bloom. Color is everywhere. Nature is as pretty as a picture. Make your own art from things that you find outside during the summer. Collect the objects that you discover, such as leaves, stones, shells, flowers, bark, and sticks. Then, make a colorful collage from your treasures.

Head outside with paper and pencil. Look around and list the things that you see, such as a bush, a tree, an ant, a cat, a sidewalk, a bee, a mailbox, a car, and a street. Sort the words into categories. Try to think of at least three ways to sort your words. For example, you could sort the words by their beginning sounds or by whether they name living or nonliving things.

Make a wind chime. Cut five or six pieces of string about as long as your arm. Tie old keys, bolts, and washers to the ends of the strings. Tie the other ends of the strings to a hanger. Use the hanger hook to hang your wind chime.

▶ Count the objects. Solve each problem.

1. Darrell has 3 cookies.
He eats 2 cookies.
How many cookies are left?

3 – 2 = _____

2. There are 6 bananas.
Pablo eats 3 bananas.
How many bananas are left?

6 – 3 = _____

3. There are 7 rabbits.
Four rabbits hop away.
How many rabbits are left?

7 – 4 = _____

4. There are 5 flowers.
Emma picks 2 flowers.
How many flowers are left?

5 – 2 = _____

Get twelve small objects that will not be harmed if they get wet. Put the objects you think will float in one pile and the objects you think will sink in another pile. With an adult, fill a bowl with water and test each item to see if it will sink or float.

▶ **Write words to describe each object.**

1. ice cream

2. watermelon

_____   _____

_____   _____

_____   _____

_____   _____

_____   _____

_____   _____

Use sidewalk chalk to draw a path of circles. Make the circles far enough away from each other that you have to jump to get from one circle to the next. When you are done, follow your path, jumping from circle to circle.

101

▶ **Unscramble each sentence. Write the words in the correct order.**

1. sun shine today will The.

    _____

2. mile today I a walked.

    _____

3. fence We painted our.

    _____

4. me knit will She something for.

    _____

Make a bowling game using six liter-sized soda bottles for the pins. Set up the six bottles any way you want. Use any large ball for the bowling ball — a basketball would work well. Each pin is worth five points. Count by fives to add up your score after each roll.

► **Write the words from the word bank in alphabetical order.**

big	stop	little	out	slow	up	go	fast

1. _____

2. _____

3. _____

4. _____

5. _____

6. _____

7. _____

8. _____

Draw a tic-tac-toe grid on a napkin or paper towel. Instead of "X"s and "O"s, use two different small-sized snacks, such as fish-shaped crackers, o-shaped cereal, bear-shaped graham crackers, carrot wheels, or grapes. Play tic-tac-toe with a friend or family member. The winner gets to eat the snacks!

▶ **Circle the greater number in each set.**

1. 17 or 71

2. 91 or 19

3. 67 or 72

4. 34 or 30

5. 26 or 41

6. 29 or 40

7. 90 or 99

8. 79 or 80

9. 44 or 54

10. 59 or 61

Play balloon soccer. Try to keep a large balloon in the air by tapping it with any part of your body except your hands. Count how many times you can touch the balloon before it touches the floor.

► **Circle the word that names each picture. Write the word on the line.**

1. 　　glove
　　　　　　　　　　　　glue

_____

2. 　　frog
　　　　　　　　　　　　flag

_____

3. 　　clown
　　　　　　　　　　　　clock

_____

4. 　　bow
　　　　　　　　　　　　bowl

_____

 Fill a jar or cup with pennies, dried beans, buttons, or some other small objects. Guess how many objects are in the jar. Check your guess by counting the objects. One easy way to count a large number of objects is to put them into groups of ten and then count the groups by ten.

105

▶ **Read each paragraph. Circle the letter of the best title.**

1. Carlos is at bat. He hits the ball. He runs to first base and then to second base. Will Carlos make it all the way to home plate?

   A. Running

   B. Carlos Likes to Play

   C. Carlos's Baseball Game

2. Madison put on sunscreen and sunglasses. Then, she found her favorite green hat. Madison was ready to go outside.

   A. A Rainy Day

   B. Ready to Go Out in the Sun

   C. Madison Likes to Play

Make a tower using paper cups and plates. Start with a paper cup, and then put a small paper plate on top of it. Next, add a cup, then another plate. How tall can you make your tower before it falls down?

106

► **Add -s or -es to make each word plural. Write the new words.**

1. hand _____

2. kitten _____

3. glass _____

4. inch _____

5. car _____

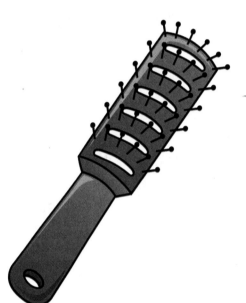

6. clock _____

7. wish _____

8. brush _____

Get a handful of change and put it on the table. Close your eyes and try to sort the coins into piles of pennies, nickels, dimes, and quarters. Open your eyes to see how you did.

► **Solve each word problem.**

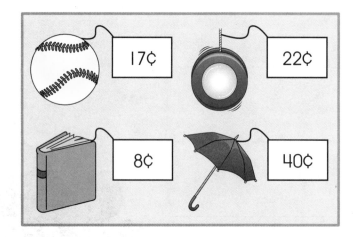

1. Lori bought an umbrella and a book. How much money did she spend?

2. Henry bought a yo-yo and an umbrella. How much money did he spend?

3. Maria bought a baseball and a yo-yo. How much money did she spend?

4. Alejandro bought a baseball and a book. How much money did he spend?

In a book or magazine, the words under or next to a picture are called captions. Cut out ten pictures and their captions from an old children's magazine. Cut off the captions. Put them in a pile on the table and mix them all up. Now, see if you can match each picture to its caption.

▶ Follow the directions to play a game of leapfrog.

Play a fun game of leapfrog to show your strength. Find a friend, sibling, or parent to join you. To play, have one person crouch down low. Have the second person place her hands on the crouching person's back and hop over him. For the first round, pretend that you are frogs. Play more rounds and transform into other hopping creatures, such as grasshoppers, rabbits, and kangaroos. Each time that you hop, remember that you are making your legs stronger and your body healthier! For a bigger strength challenge, invite friends and family members to form a line of crouching critters for you to jump over.

Choose a color word and write it at the top of a piece of paper. Draw pictures of all the foods you can think of that are that color.

▶ **Add to find each sum.**

1.   7
    + 5
	2. 8
	    + 4
		3. 7
		    + 3

4.   9
    + 5
	5. 15
	    + 2
		6. 10
		    + 6

▶ **Subtract to find each difference.**

7.   12
    − 8
	8. 9
	    − 4
		9. 11
		    − 7

10.   8
    − 8
	11. 10
	    − 2
		12. 6
		    − 2

For this activity, you will need a small piece of string, a marble, and a paper-towel tube. Make a line with the string on the carpet. Take ten steps away from the line. Now, roll your marble through the tube toward the line. Try to get as close to the line as you can without going over it.

▶ **Write the word that matches each set of clues.**

EXAMPLE:

It begins like <u>st</u>uck.

It rhymes with <u>late</u>.　　　state

1.　It begins like <u>r</u>ip.

　　It rhymes with <u>cake</u>. _____

2.　It begins like <u>t</u>iger.

　　It rhymes with <u>bag</u>. _____

3.　It begins like <u>c</u>at.

　　It rhymes with <u>ball</u>. _____

4.　It begins like <u>g</u>um.

　　It rhymes with <u>late</u>. _____

Make an animal from things you find in nature. Start with a pinecone for the body. Then, use modeling clay or glue to attach twigs, leaves, and other natural objects. Give your nature animal a name.

▶ **Write how many tens and ones.**

1. 46 = _____ tens _____ ones

2. 19 = _____ ten _____ ones

3. 84 = _____ tens _____ ones

4. 64 = _____ tens _____ ones

▶ **Write the number.**

5. 4 tens and 0 ones = _____

6. 1 ten and 1 one = _____

7. 9 tens and 3 ones = _____

8. 2 tens and 8 ones = _____

Make a picture that you can eat. Spread peanut butter or cream cheese over a piece of bread or a large cracker. Make a picture with raisins. Then, eat your picture. Yum!

▶ **Read each word. Write -s or -es to make the word plural.**

1. horse_____

2. drum_____

3. box_____

4. table_____

5. planet_____

6. bear_____

7. wish_____

8. shell_____

9. match_____

10. brick_____

11. pumpkin_____

12. glass_____

Tape two crayons together so that the points are even. Now, try writing and drawing with your double crayon!

▶ Draw the other half of the picture. Color the picture.

Any small object with a hole in it can be a bead. Collect pasta, buttons, old keys, paperclips, and other objects that could be used as beads. String them together to make an interesting necklace.

▶ **Complete each sentence to make sense.**

1. My friend _____ .

2. Will you _____ ?

3. I want _____ .

4. She went _____ .

5. The dogs _____ .

 Try this game with a friend or family member. Stick two pieces of uncooked spaghetti in a lump of modeling clay, one for you and one for your friend. Set a timer for one minute. When the time begins, start putting o-shaped cereal on the piece of spaghetti. Do not break the spaghetti, or you lose the game. The person with the most cereal on the spaghetti when the timer goes off wins.

▶ **Draw an X on each correct shape in each row. There may be more than one correct shape in each row.**

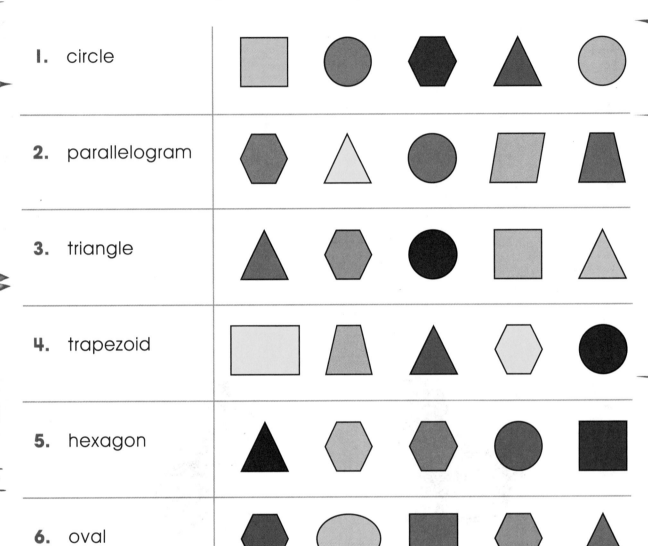

1. circle

2. parallelogram

3. triangle

4. trapezoid

5. hexagon

6. oval

Make a list of your favorite things. Include your favorite color, book, movie, sport, and food. What other favorites can you add?

▶ **Underline the misspelled word in each sentence. Then, write each misspelled word correctly on the line.**

1. What may I help yu with? _____

2. Please giv him a fork. _____

3. You can sti on the chair. _____

4. Will you miks the paint? _____

5. Noah came ovr to play. _____

Write the numbers 3, 4, 5, and 6 on the insides of four plastic bottle caps. Push the caps off the edge of a table onto the floor. The ones that land with the insides down so that you cannot see the numbers do not count. Add up the ones that land with the numbers facing up to get your score.

▶ **Which flavor of ice cream is the most popular with your friends and family? Ask each person to choose a favorite ice cream flavor from the list. Make a tally mark beside each answer given.**

vanilla _____   banana _____

chocolate _____   cherry _____

strawberry _____   other _____

_____

▶ **Count the tally marks beside each flavor. Graph your results.**

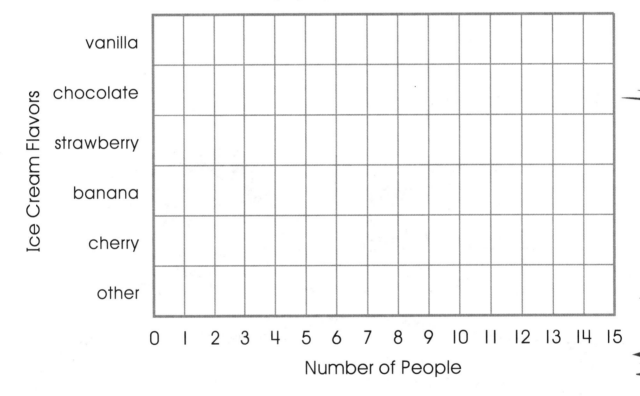

Favorite Ice Cream Flavors

Number of People

Ice Cream Flavors

Try getting dressed with your eyes closed. No peeking!

▶ **Describe the funniest dream you have ever had. Write about it below.**

_____

_____

_____

_____

_____

_____

_____

_____

_____

_____

You can make an old penny look shiny and new! Put enough vinegar in a small cup to cover a penny. Mix a couple pinches of salt into the vinegar. Drop an old penny into the cup. It should take about five minutes for your penny to get clean.

119

▶ **Read the story. Then, answer the questions.**

Morning on the Farm

Olivia lives on a farm. She wakes up early to do chores. Olivia feeds the horses and chickens. She also collects the eggs. Sometimes, she helps her dad milk the cows. Her favorite thing to do in the morning is eat breakfast.

1. Where does Olivia live? _____

   _____

2. Why does she wake up early? _____

   _____

3. Write one chore that Olivia does. _____

   _____

4. What is her favorite thing to do in the morning? _____

   _____

Many animals fly. Draw a picture of all the flying insects, birds, and mammals that you can. Now, go outside and look for some flying creatures. Make a tally chart to record how many of each kind you see.

▶ **Add to find each sum.**

1.	2 2 + 2	**2.**	1 1 + 1	**3.**	4 4 + 4
4.	5 5 + 5	**5.**	2 3 + 2	**6.**	4 3 + 0
7.	5 4 + 5	**8.**	3 3 + 3	**9.**	4 6 + 5
10.	6 4 + 2	**11.**	7 0 + 7	**12.**	10 10 + 10

You can make a sprinkler! Get an old rubber glove and cut off the finger tips. Secure the glove to the end of a hose with several strong rubber bands or string. Now, turn on the water and have fun!

▶ Follow the directions below to move like an animal.

Have you ever seen the way animals of the rain forest move? Some animals, such as monkeys and apes, swing from tree branch to tree branch. Some animals, such as sloths, slowly climb trees by stretching up and down. Read about a rain forest animal. Then, create your own stretch. Try to move like your chosen animal. Share your new stretch with a friend. Can she guess which animal you are?

Find a round object such as a bowl or flying disc that is almost as big as a piece of drawing paper. Trace around it to make a big circle. Now, find a round object that is almost as big as the one you just traced. Trace it just inside the first circle. Keep finding and tracing smaller and smaller circles until your smallest circle is the size of a penny.

▶ **Draw a line to match each pair that has the same difference.**

1. 5 – 3   5 – 1   **2.** 8 – 7   10 – 4

    8 – 3   9 – 8   3 – 1   4 – 3

    8 – 4   7 – 2   8 – 2   5 – 3

    5 – 4   6 – 4   9 – 5   7 – 3

3. 10 – 5   13 – 10   **4.** 5 – 5   14 – 7

    12 – 6   7 – 1   12 – 9   8 – 5

    2 – 0   9 – 4   11 – 4   8 – 8

    9 – 6   4 – 2   12 – 8   5 – 1

You can help birds build their nests. Find natural
objects such as twigs, reeds, and grasses that
birds could use in their nests. Put them near trees
where birds will find them. Check back every
few days to see if some of your items are missing.

▶ **Unscramble each word. Spell each word correctly on the line to complete each sentence.**

1. Juan had a _____ for _____ mother.
   igft   ihs

_____

2. The _____ has a _____ tire.
   acr   tfla

_____

3. A butterfly _____ on _____ flower.
   ats   hte

_____

4. My _____ works at the _____ .
   add   tsoer

Make a colorful design on an index card. Color
in all of the space. Use a black crayon to cover
your entire design. Now, use a paperclip to draw
through the black crayon. Your colorful design
will show through wherever you draw!

▶ **Read each paragraph. Underline the sentence that states the main idea.**

1. Sidney's umbrella is old. It has holes in it. The color is faded. It does not keep the rain off of her.

2. Tabby is a farm cat. He is tan and white. Tabby helps the farmer by catching mice in the barn. He sleeps on soft hay.

3. Big, gray clouds are in the sky. The wind is blowing, and it is getting colder. I think it will snow.

How many different sounds can you make using natural objects? Try hitting a tree with a stick, dropping a stone in water, or rustling the leaves in a tree. What other natural noises can you create?

▶ **Antonyms** are words that have opposite meanings. Write an antonym for each underlined word. Circle each antonym in the word search.

1. The opposite of <u>clean</u> is

   _____ .

2. The opposite of <u>night</u> is

   _____ .

3. The opposite of <u>hot</u> is

   _____ .

v	d	i	r	t	y	e	h	k
a	b	r	m	c	e	u	d	g
x	c	r	y	o	d	s	a	j
w	l	h	o	l	r	j	y	n
q	a	z	c	d	d	o	w	n
d	a	r	k	b	s	s	l	m
h	r	e	p	s	t	d	j	p

4. The opposite of <u>light</u> is

   _____ .

5. The opposite of <u>laugh</u> is

   _____ .

Start with the first letter of your name. Look for an object that begins with that letter. Then, look for an object that begins with the second letter. See if you can find an object for every letter in your name.

▶ **Will the figures stack flat on top of each other? Circle *yes* or *no*.**

1.

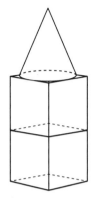

yes   no

2.

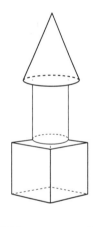

yes   no

3.

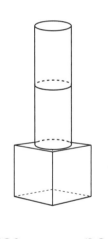

yes   no

4.

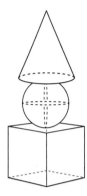

yes   no

Bring a sheet of drawing paper and some crayons outside. Choose a spot with some trees and plants. Fold your paper in half. On one side of the fold, draw the spot how it looks now. On the other side of the fold, draw how you think the spot will look during the winter.

127

▶ **Read each word. Write _e_ if the _y_ makes the long /ē/ sound, as in _story_. Write _i_ if the _y_ makes the long /ī/ sound, as in _sky_.**

1. ☐ ☐ ☐ ☐ ☐
   baby fly windy bunny fry

2. ☐ ☐ ☐ ☐ ☐
   shy family buy happy jelly

3. ☐ ☐ ☐ ☐ ☐
   cry my funny silly try

If this book could talk, what would it say? How about the chair you are sitting on? Draw a picture of an object. Add a speech bubble and write what you think the object might say if it could talk. Try drawing two objects talking to each other.

▶ **Circle the word in each row that does not belong.**

1. bean   carrot   book   lettuce   peas

2. train   jet   leg   car   boat

3. cat   orange   green   blue   red

4. lake   ocean   pond   chair   river

5. bear   apple   lion   wolf   tiger

6. Jane   Kathy   Tom   Jill   Anna

7. park   scared   happy   sad   mad

8. tulip   daffodil   rose   daisy   basket

Write down your phone number and one other phone number. If you add up all the digits in each phone number, which number do you think will have a higher total? Check your answer by adding the digits of each number.

▶ **A** fact family **is a group of addition and subtraction number sentences that have the same three numbers.**

EXAMPLE:

9	+	8	=	17		17	-	9	=	8
8	+	9	=	17		17	-	8	=	9

The numbers **8**, **9**, and **17** are used in the fact family above.

▶ **Complete each number sentence. Draw a line to match each pair of number sentences from the same fact family.**

1. 8 + 7 = _____

2. 3 + 9 = _____

3. 9 + 3 = _____

4. 7 + 8 = _____

5. 6 + 5 = _____

6. 7 + 9 = _____

7. 9 + 7 = _____

8. 5 + 6 = _____

Think of a word with five or six letters. Cut out a picture from a magazine that begins with the first letter of your word. Do the same thing for the other letters. Glue the pictures in order on a piece of paper. Explain to a friend or family member how you selected the pictures and ask if he or she can "read" your word by looking at the pictures.

▶ **Read the story. Then, answer the questions.**

Flying High

Ethan is a baby bald eagle. He is learning to fly. It has been a real **struggle** for Ethan. He has been practicing for days, but he does not seem to be improving.

Getting up in the air is easy. Flying over fields is no problem. But Ethan has trouble flying around things. He does not do well when he attempts to land on a certain spot. Perhaps he should sign up for flying lessons to improve his flying skills.

1. The word **struggle** means:

    A. something that is not easy

    B. a boat

    C. a broken wing

2. In the story, the word **he** stands for:

    A. Ethan's friend

    B. Ethan

    C. the teacher

Find a very small object. Now, find an object that is just a little bigger. Then, find an object that is just a little bigger than the last object. Keep going until you cannot find a bigger object.

▶ **Write two addition number sentences to complete each fact family. Use the same three numbers as in the subtraction number sentences.**

1.   11   −   5   =   6

         11   −   6   =   5

☐ + ☐ = ☐

☐ + ☐ = ☐

2.   14   −   6   =   8

         14   −   8   =   6

☐ + ☐ = ☐

☐ + ☐ = ☐

How much do things in your house weigh? Begin by weighing yourself on your bathroom scale. Then, try weighing yourself while you are holding an object, such as a large book, a basket of laundry, or the family cat. You can find how much the object (or animal) you are holding weighs by subtracting your weight from the weight you got when you were holding it.

▶ **Write the correct verb from below each line to complete each sentence.**

1. Amelia _____ a song.
   sing   sang

2. Did the bell _____ yet?
   ring   rang

3. The grass _____ green.
   is   are

4. She _____ a race.
   run   ran

5. Mom will _____ a short trip.
   took   take

6. Chris _____ a new scooter.
   has   have

 Find three objects that belong together and one that does not. For example, you could find a fork, a spoon, a butter knife, and a cup. Show your objects to a friend or family member and ask if that person can figure out which object does not belong.

▶ **If you could plant a garden, what would you plant and why?**

_____

_____

_____

_____

_____

_____

_____

_____

_____

You can make a magnet out of a metal paper clip. Just rub the paper clip across a magnet about 50 times. Make sure you rub in only one direction. Now, see if you can use the paper clip to pick up small metal items.

▶ **See how many words you can print that rhyme with** *pan*. **Try to add different letters to -***an* **on your own. Use the letter bank to help you.**

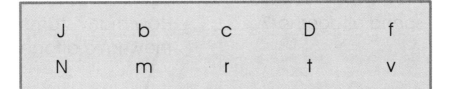

J	b	c	D	f
N	m	r	t	v

1. _____ 2. _____

3. _____ 4. _____

5. _____ 6. _____

7. _____ 8. _____

9. _____ 10. _____

How many windows are in your house? Start by picturing each window in your mind and counting all of them. Then, walk around your house and count the windows to check your guess.

▶ **Solve each word problem.**

1. Cara spent 18¢. Danielle spent 10¢. How much did they spend altogether?

2. Pilar has 10 stamps. Edward has 15 stamps. How many stamps do they have altogether?

3. Nelan has 16 fish. Jay has 12 fish. How many fish do they have in all?

4. Emily has 13 balloons. Jessi has 10 balloons. How many balloons do they have in all?

How quickly can you stack ten cups into a pyramid? Use a stopwatch and time yourself to find out.

▶ **Unscramble each word. Spell each word correctly on the line. Use the word bank to help you.**

crop	frog	glad	land
most	sled	stone	swim

1. grof _____

2. nald _____

3. etsno _____

4. lgda _____

5. stom _____

6. prco _____

7. miws _____

8. desl _____

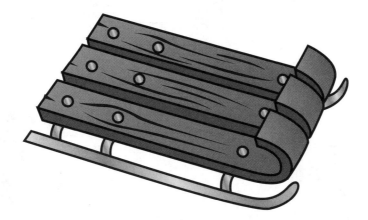

You can use a drop of water as a magnifying glass. Put a drop of water on a piece of clear plastic, like the lid to a plastic container. Now, position the plastic over the small print in a magazine or newspaper article. The water will make the print look bigger!

▶ **Add to find each sum. Draw a line to match each dog to the correct bone.**

1.
$$\begin{array}{r} 32 \\ + 21 \\ \hline \end{array}$$

2.
$$\begin{array}{r} 44 \\ + 13 \\ \hline \end{array}$$

79

53

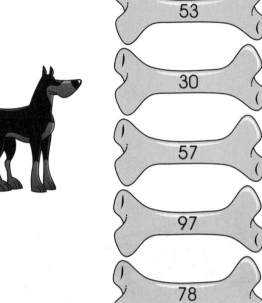

3.
$$\begin{array}{r} 73 \\ + 24 \\ \hline \end{array}$$

30

57

4.
$$\begin{array}{r} 52 \\ + 26 \\ \hline \end{array}$$

97

5.
$$\begin{array}{r} 20 \\ + 10 \\ \hline \end{array}$$

78

6.
$$\begin{array}{r} 61 \\ + 18 \\ \hline \end{array}$$

Write your name in rocks. Gather 30 or 40 rocks that are all about the same size. Use them to form the letters of your name on the ground.

► **Say the name of each picture. Circle the letters that make each ending sound.**

1.

th   sh   ch

2.

th   sh   ch

3.

th   sh   ch

4.

th   sh   ch

Write the first names of eight people you know on index cards, one name on each card. Divide them into groups by how many syllables each name has. Next, put them in order starting with the name that has the fewest letters and ending with the name that has the most. Finally, put them in alphabetical order.

139

► **Follow the directions to complete each number line.**

► **Count by 2s.**

1.

2   4   6   _____   _____   _____

► **Count by 4s.**

2.

4   _____   12   _____   _____   _____

► **Count by 5s.**

3.

5   _____   15   _____   _____   30

Ask your parents or grandparents to tell you what countries your family comes from. Then, see if you can find those countries on a map or globe.

▶ **Answer each question using a word from the word bank.**

go	tall	no	far

1. Write the word that means the opposite of <u>near</u>.

   _____

2. Write the word that means the opposite of <u>yes</u>.

   _____

3. Write the word that means the opposite of <u>stop</u>.

   _____

4. Write the word that means the opposite of <u>short</u>.

   _____

You can use a spoon as a launch pad. Go outside and set the spoon on a table right side up. Put a mini-marshmallow, fish-shaped cracker, button, or other small object on the end of the spoon handle. Press down hard on the end of the bowl part of the spoon to send your object flying. You can use a cup as a target.

▶ **Sometimes a number is added to itself. These number sentences are called** doubles facts**.**

> **EXAMPLE:**
>
> $5 + 5 = 10$ $8 + 8 = 16$

▶ **Complete the doubles facts.**

1. $7 + 7 = \boxed{}$

2. $2 + \boxed{} = 4$

3. $5 + \boxed{} = 10$

4. $4 + 4 = \boxed{}$

5. $10 + 10 = \boxed{}$

6. $9 + \boxed{} = 18$

7. $1 + \boxed{} = 2$

8. $\boxed{} + 4 = 8$

9. $\boxed{} + 7 = 14$

10. $3 + 3 = \boxed{}$

You have grown and learned a lot over the past year! Make a list of ten things you can do now that you could not do a year ago.

► **Write the correct homophone for each underlined word. Use the word bank to help you.**

bee	eight	hear	knot
right	sea	through	wood

1. Denise <u>ate</u> _____ small pancakes for breakfast.

2. Stay <u>here</u> and you can _____ the music.

3. Can you <u>see</u> the _____ from the top of the hill?

4. <u>Be</u> careful when you catch a _____!

5. <u>Would</u> you get some _____ for the fire?

6. Did you <u>write</u> the _____ answer?

7. He <u>threw</u> the ball _____ the hoop.

8. The man could <u>not</u> tie a _____ in the rope.

Have you ever noticed the boxes that are near the tops of some electrical poles? They are called pole transformers. They make sure that each house does not get too much electricity. Next time you are traveling in the car, try counting the pole transformers you see.

▶ **Have you ever helped someone without the person knowing? How did it make you feel? Describe how it felt to help someone.**

_____

_____

_____

_____

_____

_____

_____

_____

_____

Get eight plastic containers of different sizes with matching lids. Make sure none of the lids are the same size. Take the lids off the containers and mix them up. Now, close your eyes and try to put each lid on the right container.

▶ **Rearrange the letters in the phrase** *camping trip* **to make new words. Write the words on the lines.**

camping trip

_____ _____

_____ _____

_____ _____

_____ _____

_____ _____

_____ _____

Start this activity in the morning. Choose a window in your house and draw exactly what you see outside. Come back to your window a few hours later and draw what you see again. Do the same thing one or two more times. At the end of the day, compare your pictures to see how the view from your window changed throughout the day.

▶ **Draw a line to divide each compound word into two words. Write the two words on the line.**

1. goldfish

   _____

2. popcorn

   _____

3. daytime

   _____

4. doghouse

   _____

5. spaceship

   _____

6. railroad

   _____

7. blueberry

   _____

8. sailboat

   _____

9. grapefruit

   _____

10. cupcake

   _____

Sprinkle some dry oatmeal or puffed cereal on a plate. Blow up a balloon and rub it on your hair for about 10 seconds. Next, hold the balloon just above the oatmeal or cereal. Watch as it jumps onto the balloon!

► **Subtract to find each difference.**

1. 10
− 2

2. 10
− 9

3. 10
− 7

4. 10
− 1

5. 10
− 8

6. 10
− 6

7. 10
− 3

8. 11
− 9

9. 11
− 7

10. 11
− 2

11. 11
− 8

12. 11
− 4

13. 11
− 3

14. 12
− 2

15. 12
− 9

16. 12
− 1

How many math problems can you make using only the numbers *1*, *2*, *3*, *4*, and *5*? You can use addition and subtraction, and you can use the same number more than once. You cannot use any number bigger than *5*, even for the answer.

► **Synonyms** are words that have the same meanings. **Antonyms** are words that have opposite meanings. Underline the synonym and circle the antonym for the first word in each row.

1.	big	large	little	dog
2.	fast	slow	car	quick
3.	glad	silly	sad	happy
4.	smile	grin	mouth	frown
5.	sunny	bright	cloudy	play
6.	cold	chilly	hot	joy
7.	quiet	loud	boy	silent

Make a map of your bedroom. First, draw an outline that is the shape of your room. Then, draw the furniture as if you were looking down on it from above. Be sure to show where the door and windows are. Remember to label your map.

▶ **Number the sentences in the order that the events happened.**

I. _____ Jenny made a chocolate cake for her friend.

2. _____ Jenny put blue frosting on the cake.

3. _____ Jenny put sprinkles on the cake.

4. _____ Jenny went to the store and bought a box of cake mix.

▶ **Draw and color a picture of the cake that Jenny made.**

Try this trick to fool your friends. Put a heavy rock in the corner of a cardboard box. Put the lid on the box. Now, balance the corner of the box with the rock inside on the edge of a table. Your friends will wonder why the box does not fall!

▶ Follow the directions below to make the world a better place.

Integrity means that you always do the right thing, even when no one is watching. Having integrity is always doing what you feel is right whether you are in front of a group, with one person, or alone. On a separate sheet of paper, write what you would do in the following situation:

You helped start a school recycling program because you know that taking care of the earth is important. You are outside when you finish your granola bar, and you do not see a trash can anywhere. What do you do with the wrapper?

Try this memory game. Walk around your yard or a park and touch five different things, such as a bush, a bench, a jump rope, a ball, and a hose. Then, walk around again and touch the same five things in the same order. If five is too easy, try adding more. You can play this game alone or with a friend.

▶ **Color the balloon whose number matches each description. Use the color listed.**

1.

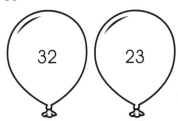

2 tens and 3 ones
blue

2.

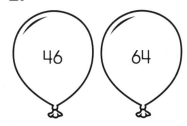

4 tens and 6 ones
green

3.

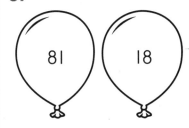

I ten and 8 ones
purple

4.

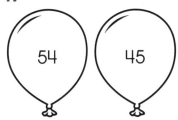

5 tens and 4 ones
orange

5.

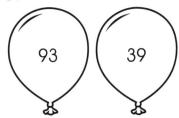

3 tens and 9 ones
black

6.

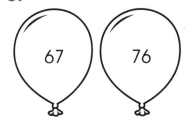

6 tens and 7 ones
brown

Get some crayons and paper. Then, put on some music. Draw how the music makes you feel. Try a different kind of music. Does different music make you want to draw differently?

► **In each sentence, one word is misspelled. Write the correctly spelled word from the word bank on the line.**

barn	help	pet	wet

1. A dog is a good pat.

_____

2. The horse sleeps in the banr.

_____

3. She ran to get hilp.

_____

4. The paper got wit.

_____

Make a ramp by leaning a board on a stack of books. Roll a toy car down the ramp and put a marker on the floor at the place where it stops. Then, add a book to make the ramp higher. What happens when you roll the car down the ramp again?

► **Read each sentence. Circle each noun. A noun can be a person, place, or thing.**

1. The boy lost his shoe.

2. She wrote a letter to her aunt.

3. Did you have a sandwich?

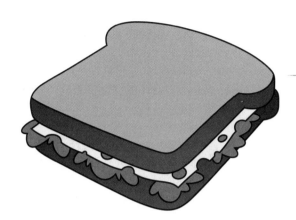

4. We saw a movie about butterflies.

5. My little sister has a brown teddy bear.

6. The girl wore a blue shirt.

7. I am going to the store with my mom.

Write a kind note to someone in your family. Hide the note in a place where only that person will find it. Did your kind note brighten someone's day?

153

► **Write the months of the year in order.**

October	July	January
December	May	April
August	February	June
March	November	September

_____   _____

_____   _____

_____   _____

_____   _____

_____   _____

_____   _____

Bring some paper and a pencil outside. Choose a flower, fern, or small bush to draw. Try to make your drawing look as much like the plant as you can. Then label the parts of the plant.

► **Complete each sentence using words from the word bank.**

swing	jump	walk
run	ride	swim

1. I like to _____ my bike.

2. My sister loves to _____ high at the park.

3. Nick can _____ like a frog.

4. At the pool, I like to _____ .

5. I _____ in a single file line at school.

6. Kelly can _____ very fast.

Ask a friend or family member to write down four words. Write a poem using all four of the words. Illustrate it.

► **Circle the odd numbers in each row.**

1. 2   5   7   3   9   4   6   11   14

2. 1   10   6   7   12   13   15   2   17

3. 5   11   9   13   14   17   19   3   8

► **Circle the even numbers in each row.**

4. 6   9   2   11   4   7   3   8   12

5. 13   8   10   6   12   16   9   5   19

6. 14   16   9   11   12   18   7   4   8

Fill a tub or wading pool with water outside. Get several objects that will not be harmed if they get wet. Stand up tall and drop each object into the water. Listen for the sound each object makes. What makes the loudest sounding splash, and what makes the softest?

► **Write the missing consonant in each word.**

1.

ca____el

2.

se____en

3.

ti____er

4.

spi____er

5.

le____on

6.

ru____er

Start a collection of items you find in nature, such as rocks, shells, feathers, acorns, and pinecones. Display them in an empty egg carton, or use a shoe box if your items are big.

157

▶ **Write the correct punctuation mark at the end of each sentence. Use a . or ?.**

1. Have you been to the circus_____

2. We went on Saturday_____

3. We saw monkeys_____

4. Would you like to be a clown_____

5. We ate lots of fluffy, pink cotton candy_____

6. Have you ever had a candy apple_____

7. It is my favorite thing to eat_____

Where do the books go when you put them in the book drop? Next time you are at the library, ask the librarian to show you what happens to the books after they go down the book drop chute.

158

► **Say the name of each picture. Write the vowels to complete each word.**

1.

c_____ _____n

2.

c_____ _____l

3.

_____ _____l

4.

b_____ _____l

Do you have a broken alarm clock, telephone, radio, or calculator at home? Ask an adult if you can take it apart to see what is inside. Use a screwdriver to take off the plastic cover. If there are a lot of small parts, you can put them in an empty egg carton. What can you learn about how the machine worked?

159

► **Invent and design a new kind of juice box. Draw your design below. Describe your new juice box on a separate sheet of paper.**

You will need an old pair of gloves for this activity. Ask an adult to cut off the fingers close to the palm part of the glove. Decorate the fingers to make finger puppets.

▶ **Read the passage. Answer the questions.**

Black-Footed Ferrets

Years ago, many black-footed ferrets lived in the American West. They were wild and free. Their habitat was the flat grasslands. This habitat was destroyed by humans.

The ferrets began to vanish. Almost all of them died. Scientists worked to save the ferrets' lives. Now, the number of ferrets has increased.

1. Where did the black-footed ferrets live? _____

   _____

2. Who worked to save the ferrets? _____

   _____

3. What happened after scientists started to help the ferrets?

   _____

Start your own address book. Write down the addresses of friends and family members. Organize them in a binder or make your own book. Do not forget to put the addresses in ABC order!

161

▶ **Write *oi* or *oy* to complete each word. Write the word on the line.**

1. b_____ _____

   _____

2. t_____ _____

   _____

3. s_____ _____l

   _____

4. p_____ _____nt

   _____

5. _____ _____ster

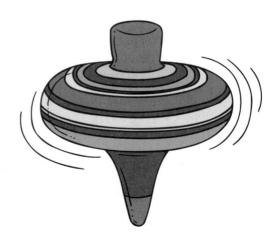

   _____

6. v_____ _____ce

   _____

Some words have double letters. In fact, there is a word with double letters in this sentence! Find an article in an old magazine. Circle all the words with double letters you can find.

▶ **Write the correct numbers to get the answer in each box.**

1. $4 - \rule{2cm}{0.4pt} =$

$3 + \rule{2cm}{0.4pt} =$ $\boxed{3}$

$2 + \rule{2cm}{0.4pt} =$

2. $5 + \rule{2cm}{0.4pt} =$

$2 + \rule{2cm}{0.4pt} =$ $\boxed{6}$

$9 - \rule{2cm}{0.4pt} =$

3. $7 + \rule{2cm}{0.4pt} =$

$\rule{2cm}{0.4pt} - 1 =$ $\boxed{8}$

$\rule{2cm}{0.4pt} - 3 =$

4. $\rule{2cm}{0.4pt} - 4 =$

$8 - \rule{2cm}{0.4pt} =$ $\boxed{5}$

$3 + \rule{2cm}{0.4pt} =$

Most of the time, we look at trees from the side. To look at a tree in a different way, lie on your back under a tree. Look up into the branches. How is this view different from when you are standing up?

► **Write the correct word to complete each sentence.**

1. A dime is a_____ .
   coin   coyn

2. I want to buy my friend a new _____ .
   toi   toy

3. My cat has one white _____ .
   paw   pau

4. Dan has two sons and one_____ .
   daughter   dawter

5. The water in the pan started to _____ .
   boyl   boil

6. The _____ was very silly.
   clown   cloun

Hop on one foot until you lose your balance.
Count your hops. Now, hop on the other foot
and count your hops. Which foot was easier to
hop on?

▶ **Write the correct contractions.**

1. cannot _____

2. I am _____

3. you are _____

4. do not _____

5. he is _____

▶ **Write the two words in each contraction.**

6. didn't _____

7. isn't _____

8. you've _____

9. she's _____

10. couldn't _____

Put small, light objects, such as corks, packing peanuts, or popped popcorn on a table or bench outside. Use the stream of water from a spray bottle to knock them over. How far away can you stand and still hit the targets?

▶ **Write the number of tens and ones in each number.**

1.
20

tens	ones

2.
16

tens	ones

3.
14

tens	ones

4.
31

tens	ones

5.
22

tens	ones

6.
12

tens	ones

7.
47

tens	ones

8.
24

tens	ones

9.
36

tens	ones

10.
55

tens	ones

11.
11

tens	ones

12.
63

tens	ones

Get a handful of change. See how many ways you can make 50¢. Whenever you find a new way, write it down on a piece of paper using this code: *P*=penny, *N*=nickel, *D*=dime, *Q*=quarter.

▶ **Write *is* or *are* to complete each sentence.**

1. We _____ going to town tomorrow.

2. This book _____ not mine.

3. Where _____ a box of cereal?

4. Seals _____ fast swimmers.

5. _____ he planning to help?

6. _____ you going to the festival?

▶ **Write a sentence using *is*.**

_____

▶ **Write a sentence using *are*.**

_____

Fold a piece of paper in half. Write "Rough" on one side of the fold and "Smooth" on the other side. Take your paper outside and look for things that are rough and smooth. Draw each thing on the correct side of your paper.

167

► **Write the correct punctuation mark at the end of each sentence. Use ., !, or ?.**

1. Are we going to the park_____

2. Look out for the ball_____

3. I know you can do it_____

4. Do bulls have horns on their heads_____

5. The girl on the bike is my sister _____

6. We won the game _____

7. The store is two blocks away _____

Cut a picture out of a magazine and glue it to a piece of paper. In the space around the picture, write words that describe it. Write as many words as you can.

▶ **Subtract to find each difference.**

1. 15
   − 4

2. 14
   − 2

3. 16
   − 8

4. 17
   − 3

5. 13
   − 4

6. 10
   − 4

7. 18
   − 7

8. 13
   − 6

9. 11
   − 9

10. 16
    − 5

11. 12
    − 2

12. 19
    − 6

Draw a circle, a triangle, and a rectangle at the top of a piece of paper. Walk around with your paper and a pencil. Every time you see one of those shapes, make a tally mark under the shape.

169

▶ **Write the two words that make up each compound word.**

1. doghouse   _____ + _____

2. football   _____ + _____

3. fishbowl   _____ + _____

4. sandbox   _____ + _____

5. rainbow   _____ + _____

6. baseball   _____ + _____

7. pancake   _____ + _____

8. firefighter   _____ + _____

Have a backwards day. Wear your clothes backwards. Walk backwards. Eat dinner for breakfast and breakfast for lunch. What other backwards things can you do?

▶ **Find a synonym in the word bank for each word. Write the synonym on the line.**

angry	big	close	happy
ill	quick	start	tidy

1. begin _____

2. shut _____

3. sick _____

4. mad _____

5. glad _____

6. neat _____

7. large _____

8. fast _____

Go outside and look for a wild animal, such as an insect, bird, or squirrel. Draw a food web showing what that animal eats and what it is eaten by.

171

▶ **Circle the scrambled word in each sentence. Spell each word correctly on the line.**

1. A brzea is an animal with stripes. _____

2. The robin has nowlf away. _____

3. We mixed flour and oil in a owlb. _____

4. Button your button and zip your rpzipe. _____

5. A lot of leppeo were at the playground. _____

6. We met our new neighbors yatdo. _____

7. My old oessh do not fit. _____

8. We played at the karp. _____

Go on a dictionary hunt! Look through a children's dictionary. What is the longest word? Shortest? Funniest?

▶ **Follow the directions below to get fit anytime.**

Your favorite playground can become your personal gym! Get on the monkey bars and carry yourself across for a great arm and upper-body workout. Use a park bench to hold your feet while you do sit-ups to increase your core strength. Exercise does not have to feel like work. Just play hard, be creative, and have fun. Think of ways to challenge yourself, and you will build your strength.

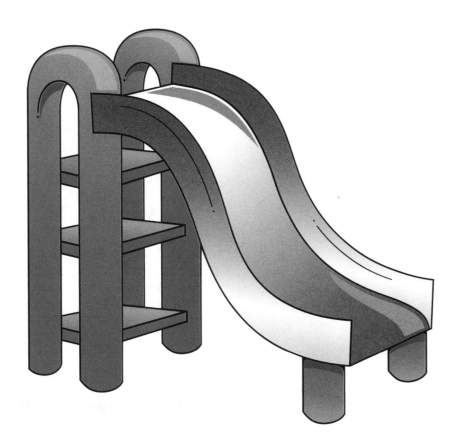

Put two rubber bands around a jar, one near the top and one near the bottom. Find about twenty twigs a little bigger than your jar. Tuck the twigs under the rubber bands to make an interesting twig-covered vase.

▶ **Add to find each sum.**

1. 3
    5
    + 2

2. 6
    4
    + 3

3. 9
    2
    + 2

4. 5
    1
    + 2

5. 4
    3
    + 4

6. 2
    3
    + 5

7. 4
    5
    + 3

8. 7
    2
    + 1

9. 1
    8
    + 1

10. 6
    1
    + 4

11. 2
    3
    + 2

12. 8
    2
    + 3

Cut out coupons from the newspaper or coupon flyers your family gets in the mail. Sort them in groups by what they are used to buy. Put each group of coupons in an envelope, and write what kind of coupons are inside on the front. Next time your family goes grocery shopping, you can bring your coupon envelopes to help your family save some money.

▶ **Write the two words that make each compound word.**

1. fingernail _____ + _____

2. treehouse _____ + _____

3. airplane _____ + _____

4. swimsuit _____ + _____

5. raindrop _____ + _____

6. basketball _____ + _____

7. sandbox _____ + _____

8. fishbowl _____ + _____

Go on a scent walk outside. Bring paper and a pencil. Write down everything you smell. If you smell a scent and do not know what it is, put a question mark on your paper. How many different scents can you find?

▶ **Find a synonym in the word bank for each underlined word. Write the synonym on the line.**

automobile	rush
glad	small

1. The ladybug is very <u>tiny</u>. _____

2. The <u>car</u> ran out of gas. _____

3. Casey won, so he was very <u>happy</u>. _____

4. My uncle was in a big <u>hurry</u>. _____

Make a rebus story by writing a story and then replacing some of the words with small pictures. For example, instead of writing, "Then the monkey ate the banana," you could replace the word "monkey" with a picture of a monkey and the word "banana" with a picture of a banana. When you are done, ask a friend or family member to read your story out loud.

▶ **Circle the pictures that have the long /ō/ vowel sound.**

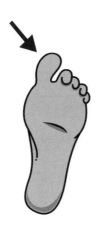

▶ **Match each word to the correct picture. Draw the ‾ symbol above the long vowel.**

1. globe

2. notes

3. boat

Draw a line on the pavement with sidewalk chalk. With a piece of chalk in your hand, stand behind the line and jump as far as you can. Mark the spot you jumped to with your chalk. Now, use a tape measure to see how far you jumped!

▶ Read the stories below. Write the main idea of each story in the space provided.

Joe had a birthday party. He invited his friends. He got presents. He ate cake and ice cream.

_____

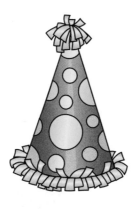 

Teena wore a costume. She went from house to house. People gave her candy. It was Halloween.

_____

Make a nature bracelet. Put a piece of masking tape around your wrist, sticky side out. Then, go on a walk and collect small natural objects, such as flowers, leaves, and seeds to put on the tape.

► **Color each shape to show the fraction.**

1.

$\dfrac{1}{2}$

2.

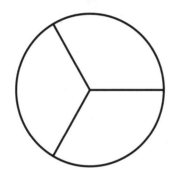

$\dfrac{1}{3}$

3.

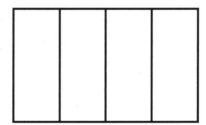

$\dfrac{1}{4}$

You can make a birdbath by putting water in a large, shallow bowl or tub. Make the water just a few inches deep so the birds will be able to stand in it. Put the tub on a picnic table near trees. Check your birdbath often to see if birds are using it.

▶ **Draw a line to match each contraction to the word pair that makes the contraction.**

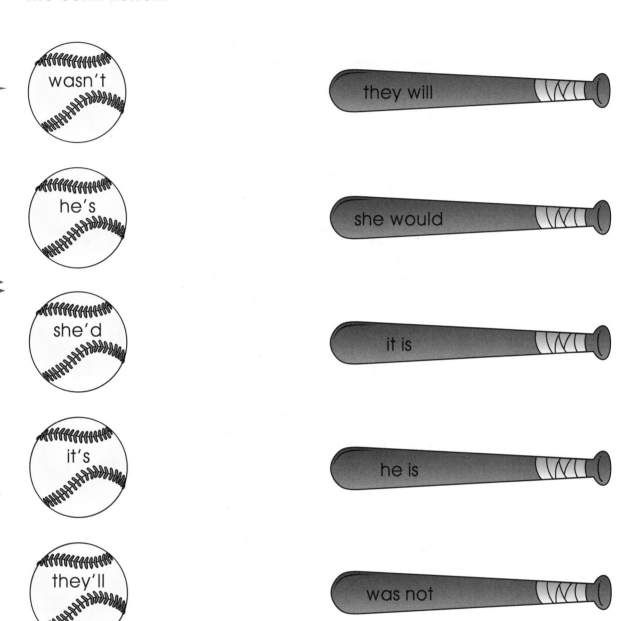

wasn't

he's

she'd

it's

they'll

they will

she would

it is

he is

was not

Get eight different cans of food from your kitchen. Put them in ABC order. Then, put them in order starting with the food you like the best and ending with the food you like the least.

▶ **Read each sentence. Underline the word that completes each sentence. Circle the beginning blend.**

1. Be careful, the road is_____ .   glue   slippery   cloudy

2. John likes to _____ trees.   blare   flower   climb

3. We will go _____ in the backyard.   gloom   play   blue

4. Mom uses _____ to make a cake.   plants   flour   clothes

_____

▶ **Write three words that each begin with a different blend:** *bl-*, *cl-*, *fl-*, *gl-*, *pl-*, **or** *sl-*.

5. _____

6. _____

7. _____

Is your family's phone number in the phonebook? Find out by looking it up. You will need to use the white pages, not the yellow pages. How many other people in your town have the same last name as you?

▶ **Solve each problem.**

1. $\begin{array}{r} 71 \\ +\ 7 \\ \hline \end{array}$	**2.** $\begin{array}{r} 48 \\ +\ 1 \\ \hline \end{array}$	**3.** $\begin{array}{r} 32 \\ +\ 7 \\ \hline \end{array}$	**4.** $\begin{array}{r} 53 \\ -\ 3 \\ \hline \end{array}$
5. $\begin{array}{r} 17 \\ -\ 2 \\ \hline \end{array}$	**6.** $\begin{array}{r} 90 \\ +\ 6 \\ \hline \end{array}$	**7.** $\begin{array}{r} 23 \\ +\ 5 \\ \hline \end{array}$	**8.** $\begin{array}{r} 64 \\ -\ 3 \\ \hline \end{array}$
9. $\begin{array}{r} 85 \\ +\ 3 \\ \hline \end{array}$	**10.** $\begin{array}{r} 72 \\ +\ 4 \\ \hline \end{array}$	**11.** $\begin{array}{r} 42 \\ -\ 1 \\ \hline \end{array}$	**12.** $\begin{array}{r} 67 \\ +\ 2 \\ \hline \end{array}$

Put some paperclips in a glass of water. Move a magnet along the outside of the glass to make the paperclips "swim."

► **Unscramble each word. Spell each word correctly on the line.**

1. ribd _____

2. eack _____

3. nebo _____

4. lebl _____

5. gbrni _____

6. ithkn _____

7. oonn _____

8. ppayh _____

9. seay _____

10. dbyo _____

Use a funnel to fill a clear liter soda bottle about ¾ full of uncooked rice. Put eight to ten small objects in the bottle. Some ideas include marbles, paper clips, dried lima beans, pen caps, acorns, dice, or small rocks. Put the cap on the bottle and shake it so that the rice covers all of the objects. Now, try to find the objects again by moving the bottle.

183

▶ **Write the missing numerals in each row.**

1. 51, _____ , 53, 54, 55, _____ , 57, _____

2. 58, 59, _____ , 61, _____ , 63, 64, 65 _____

3. 66, 67, _____ , 69, _____ , 71, 72, 73, _____

4. 74, _____ , 76, 77, _____ , 79, 80, 81, _____

5. 83, 84, 85, _____ , _____ , 88, 89, _____ , 91

Write the full names of all your family members.
Whose name has the fewest letters? Whose
name has the most?

▶ **Circle the pictures that have the long /ū/ vowel sound.**

▶ **Use a word from the word bank to complete each sentence. Draw the ‾ symbol above the long vowel u.**

tune	mule	tube

1. The _____ was inside the barn.

2. The boy played a _____ on the piano.

3. The toothpaste was in a _____ .

Without looking, write down everything you can think of that is behind you. When you are done with your list, turn around and see if you missed anything.

185

▶ An **adjective** is a word that describes a person, place, or thing. Write the best adjective from the word bank to complete each sentence.

funny	furry	hard	oak	red	six

1. His kite got caught in that _____ tree.

2. I cannot believe you ate _____ apples.

3. We laughed at the _____ clowns.

4. Kayley got a _____ bike from her parents.

5. My pillow is very _____ and lumpy.

6. The rabbits all have soft and _____ ears.

Write a word in big letters on a piece of paper. Glue dried beans on the letters so that the word is made from the beans. When the glue dries, ask a friend or family member to "read" the word by feeling it with her fingers, with eyes closed.

► **Add to find each sum.**

1. 9 + 5 = _____

2. 7 + 6 = _____

3. 8 + 3 = _____

4. 7 + 3 = _____

5. 9 + 7 = _____

6. 8 + 5 = _____

7. $\begin{array}{r} 9 \\ + 9 \\ \hline \end{array}$

8. $\begin{array}{r} 8 \\ + 4 \\ \hline \end{array}$

9. $\begin{array}{r} 6 \\ + 5 \\ \hline \end{array}$

10. $\begin{array}{r} 8 \\ + 7 \\ \hline \end{array}$

11. $\begin{array}{r} 7 \\ + 5 \\ \hline \end{array}$

12. $\begin{array}{r} 9 \\ + 8 \\ \hline \end{array}$

Write the name of eight different colors on sticky notes. Then, take your sticky notes to your room and post each sticky note on an object that matches the color you wrote.

187

▶ **Write the word. Draw the ˘ symbol over the short vowel sound.**

1. _____ 2. _____ 3. _____

_____

▶ **Read the words. Draw an X on the word that does not make the ă sound.**

4.	land	cab	name	back	cat
5.	tag	base	dad	pal	ant
6.	snake	bat	plant	tan	van

Choose a letter from your name. Write it at the top of a piece of paper. Look carefully at every part of a box of cereal. Whenever you see your letter, make a tally mark on your paper. Try it again with another letter. Which letter has the most tally marks?

▶ **Circle the coins that add up to the amount shown.**

1. 10¢

5¢   5¢

5¢   5¢

2. 16¢

5¢   10¢

1¢   1¢   10¢

3. 25¢

5¢   5¢

1¢   10¢   10¢

4. 45¢

10¢   5¢

10¢   10¢   10¢

Metal objects that stick to magnets can become magnets themselves. Stick a paperclip onto a magnet. Then, stick a second paperclip onto the first one without letting the second paperclip touch the magnet. Can you add a third paperclip to the chain? How about a fourth?

▶ **Draw a line to match each pair of homophones.**

1. ate   one

2. cent   hour

3. our   sent

4. won   new

5. knew   eight

6. pair   blue

7. hear   pear

8. know   write

9. right   here

10. blew   no

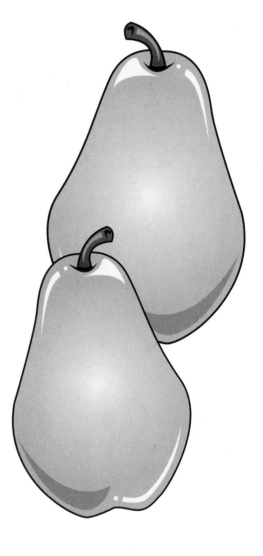

How do you know what direction the wind is blowing? Go on a wind walk. When you feel the wind, look for clues, such as leaves blowing or flowers bending. Is anything being carried away by the wind?

► **Circle the blend at the beginning of each word. Say the word.**

1. proud

2. brain

3. dress

4. crest

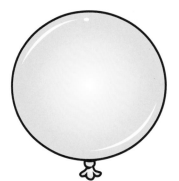

5. greet

6. track

7. free

8. drag

9. trampoline

10. crack

11. pretend

12. bring

13. dream

14. brown

15. groom

16. frozen

How many different parts are in a flower? Pick a flower. Pull off the petals and put them on one spot of a piece of paper. Label the spot "petals." Do the same thing for the leaves, stem, buds, and any other part of the flower.

191

► **Solve each problem.**

1.	10 − 4	**2.**	18 − 14	**3.**	7 − 3	**4.**	7 + 5	**5.**	8 + 2

6.	6 − 4	**7.**	9 − 4	**8.**	11 − 1	**9.**	11 + 8	**10.**	10 − 8

11. 8 + 6 = _____

12. 9 + 3 = _____

13. 4 + 9 = _____

14. 6 + 2 = _____

15. 7 + 5 = _____

16. 9 + 7 = _____

Do this activity outside! Tie the handle of a beach pail to a piece of rope a little shorter than you are. Fill the bucket half full with water. Stand away from other people and swing the pail around in a circle over your head. If you do it fast enough, the water will stay in the pail, even when it is upside down.

▶ **Draw a line to match each pair of antonyms.**

1. strong   new   8. always   short

2. bad   sad   9. light   fast

3. over   weak   10. slow   off

4. old   good   11. tall   never

5. happy   under   12. on   sink

6. add   dry   13. inside   dark

7. wet   subtract   14. float   outside

Grab a handful of a small snack, such as fish-shaped crackers, o-shaped cereal, or thin pretzel sticks. Put them on a plate or napkin. Estimate how many you have. Count by twos to check your guess. Now, eat your snack!

193

▶ **Read each sentence. Follow the directions.**

Draw a plate on a place mat.

Draw a napkin on the left side of the plate.

Draw a fork on the napkin.

Draw a knife and spoon on the right side of the plate.

Draw a glass of juice above the knife and spoon.

Draw your favorite lunch on the plate.

Find several different kinds of artificial feathers. Use your feathers as paint brushes with watercolor paints. Which type of feathers works the best for painting?

► **Complete the writing activity.**

If I could fly anywhere, I would fly to _____ because

_____

_____

_____

_____

_____

_____

_____

Cut a piece of string so that it is as long as you are. Use your string to measure objects around your house. Can you find something that is the same size that you are?

▶ What sinks to the bottom of a river first—soil, sand, or pebbles?

Materials:
- 3 paper cups
- sand
- funnel
- soda bottle (2-liter with cap)
- soil
- pebbles
- water

Procedure:

1. Fill one paper cup with soil, one cup with sand, and one cup with pebbles. These will be the sediment.

2. Use the funnel to pour the soil, sand, and pebbles into the bottle. Pour water into the bottle until it is almost full. Close the cap tightly.

3. Shake the bottle until everything is mixed well.

4. Place the bottle on a table. On a separate sheet of paper, draw a picture of what you see in the bottle. Watch as the sediment begins to settle.

5. Check the bottle after 15–30 minutes. Draw what you see.

6. Check the bottle again in 24 hours. Draw what you see.

What Is This All About?

Sediment is the soil, sand, and pebbles that wash into streams, rivers, and lakes. In nature, sediment piles up and forms sedimentary rocks.

In the bottle, you have created a small body of water with a lot of sediment. The larger pieces of sediment settle to the bottom more quickly. The smaller pieces of sediment are more likely to float in the water longer and settle to the bottom more slowly.

Use sidewalk chalk to make a long, curvy line on the ground. Try to walk along the line while balancing a book on your head.

Solve each problem. Draw a line to match the related facts.

6 + 8 = ___14___   8 + 9 = _____

13 − 4 = _____   12 − 8 = _____

15 − 8 = _____   14 − 6 = ___8___

8 + 4 = _____   7 + 8 = _____

17 − 9 = _____   9 + 4 = _____

Make a beanbag by putting dried beans into an old sock. Fill the sock only part way. Wrap string around the opening and tie it in a tight knot to keep the beans from spilling out. Use scissors to cut off the part of the sock above the string.

▶ **Did you know that you can make a taste map of your tongue?**

Materials:
- lemon (cut in half)
- pretzel
- water
- grapefruit rind
- sugar cube

Procedure:

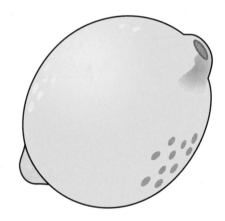

1. Touch the inside of a lemon to the very tip of your tongue. Do you taste it? Do not move your tongue around. Rinse your mouth with water. Touch the lemon to the middle of your tongue. Do you taste it? Rinse your mouth with water. Touch the lemon to the sides of your tongue. Do you taste it?

2. Rinse your mouth with water. Repeat the activity with the pretzel, the grapefruit, and the sugar cube.

What Is This All About?

There are four main tastes that humans can tell apart: sweet, sour, salty, and bitter. Your tongue is divided into different taste zones. Each taste zone is a certain area of your tongue. In this activity, you should discover which parts of your tongue detect each kind of taste.

Find five pairs of shoes. Mix them up in a big pile. Now, close your eyes and try to find matching pairs of shoes just by touching them. Can you match all five pairs of shoes without opening your eyes?

▶ Follow the directions below to make a time line of your life.

A time line is a list of dates that tells important things that have happened. You have already had a lot of things happen in your lifetime. Make a time line to show your accomplishments, milestones, and important events. Ask an adult to help you. If you have a baby book, scrapbooks, photo albums, or other records, use those things to help too. You will need a piece of poster board and markers to create the time line. List at least 10 different events to show a variety of activities. If possible, attach photos or drawings to highlight the events. This is a fun way to look back at your history. Display the time line in a special place in your bedroom. Add to it as you grow and do more.

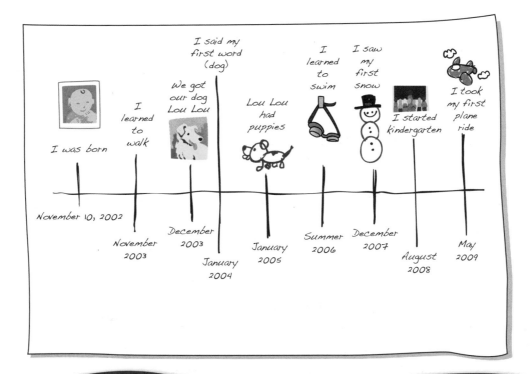

Go on a walk to look for animal homes. Look for spider webs, burrows, nests, ant hills, and other animal homes. Draw a picture of each home that you find. Remember not to get too close to the animal or its home.

▶ **Write *am*, *is*, or *are* to complete each sentence.**

1. Hannah _____ sick today.

2. Carlos _____ sick too.

3. Hannah and Carlos _____ not in school.

4. They _____ at home resting.

5. A lot of my friends _____ getting sick.

6. It seems like winter _____ a time when a lot of people get sick.

7. I _____ glad I am not sick.

8. I _____ sleeping well and eating well to help my body stay healthy.

Draw five large circles on the pavement with sidewalk chalk. Put the numbers 5, 6, 7, 8, and 9 in the circles — one number in each circle. Stand a few feet back and toss two rocks onto the circles. Find your score by adding the two circles that your rocks landed in. You can play by yourself or with a friend.

▶ **Subtract to find each difference.**

1.
$$\begin{array}{r} 29 \\ -\ 12 \\ \hline \end{array}$$

2.
$$\begin{array}{r} 45 \\ -\ 23 \\ \hline \end{array}$$

3.
$$\begin{array}{r} 99 \\ -\ 65 \\ \hline \end{array}$$

4.
$$\begin{array}{r} 87 \\ -\ 36 \\ \hline \end{array}$$

5.
$$\begin{array}{r} 87 \\ -\ 65 \\ \hline \end{array}$$

6.
$$\begin{array}{r} 64 \\ -\ 32 \\ \hline \end{array}$$

7.
$$\begin{array}{r} 76 \\ -\ 25 \\ \hline \end{array}$$

8.
$$\begin{array}{r} 39 \\ -\ 22 \\ \hline \end{array}$$

It is important to drink enough water in the summer. Decorate your water bottle with stickers. Then you will always know which bottle is yours!

201

▶ **Follow the directions below to make your own map.**

Some maps help people find their way. Other maps show physical features (things like oceans and mountains) of places. These are called relief maps. Make your own relief map in a sandbox. Get out your shovel and pail to dig and build. Be sure to make features such as a mountain, a lake, a river, a hill, an ocean, an island, a volcano, a desert, a forest, and a valley. Add water to fill up the water features. Use things that you find in nature, such as rocks, to build the mountains. Find some small sticks for trees and bushes. Soon, you will have your own real-life relief map.

Try this game of catch with a friend. Start close together. After every catch, each person must take one step back. How far apart can you get before someone drops the ball? For extra fun, try this with a water balloon.

▶ **Write the value of each set of coins.**

1. _____ ¢

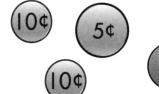

2. _____ ¢

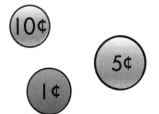

3. _____ ¢

4. _____ ¢

5. _____ ¢

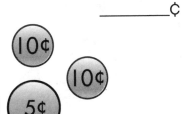

6. _____ ¢

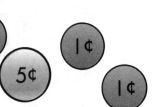

Numbers are everywhere—on clocks, food labels, keyboards, and more. Start this game by looking for a *1*. Then, look for a *2, 3, 4,* and so on. You must find the numbers in order. How far can you go before you get stuck?

▶ Follow the directions below to make a globe.

A globe is a 3-D map that shows what Earth looks like. Make your own globe with a beach ball or large plastic ball and markers. Draw a line around the middle of the ball to represent the equator. The equator is a pretend line that marks the middle of the world. Label the top of the ball *north pole* and the bottom of the ball *south pole*. The north and south poles are places that mark the top and the bottom of the earth. Draw and label the seven continents (Africa, Antarctica, Asia, Australia, Europe, North America, and South America) and the four major oceans (Arctic, Atlantic, Indian, and Pacific). Place a star sticker on the globe to represent the place where you live. Toss the globe around with a friend or family member and try to learn the names of the important places that you marked. Soon, you will know more about Earth than you did before.

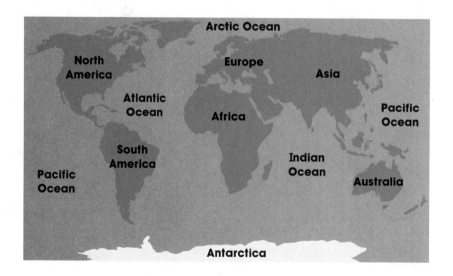

You can make sculptures from straws. Use scissors to cut plastic straws into different sizes. Put them together by squishing and folding one end of a straw and pushing it through the opening of another straw. Use thread to hang your creations.

▶ Follow the directions below for some fun outdoor activities.

Set up a safe mini-obstacle course in a grassy area. Use soft objects, such as piles of cut grass or piles of leaves. Arrange the items in a line. When you reach the end of the course, turn around and retrace your steps to repeat it. Vary the way that you go through the course, such as running, hopping, crabwalking, or skipping.

Take a friend, sibling, or parent outside with you and challenge him to a "rhyme-off." Find a spot to sit down and begin by pointing out an object that you see, such as a rose. Invite your partner to think of a real word that rhymes with *rose*, such as *nose*. (*Zose* will not work.) Go back and forth until neither of you can think of any other rhyming words. Then, pick a new outside word and start again.

Play outdoor opposites. The park is perfect for this game. While you are there, look around. Try to find opposite events that are happening. For example, you might see a sad toddler who fell when playing but a happy dog rolling in the grass. See how many opposites you can find!

Put a table tennis ball into a plastic or metal mixing bowl. Move the bowl so that the ball begins to spin around the bowl's sides. How fast can you get the ball spinning without it flying out of the bowl?

▶ **Complete each table.**

1.

Add 10	
5	15
8	
7	
9	
3	
4	

2.

Add 8	
2	
6	
4	
7	
3	
5	

3.

Add 6	
10	
6	
8	
7	
4	
5	

Have a silent day. For one day, do not talk.
Use hand gestures and writing to communicate.
If a day is too long, try it for an hour.

▶ **Circle the word that is spelled correctly in each row.**

1. ca'nt   can'nt   can't

2. esy   easy   eazy

3. kea   key   kee

4. buy   buye   biy

5. liht   light   ligte

6. wonce   onse   once

7. carry   carey   carre

8. you're   yure   yo're

9. star   stor   starr

10. funy   funny   funnie

Write a silly sentence with three rhyming words.
For example: A *fig* in a *wig* danced a *jig*.
Illustrate your sentence.

© Rainbow Bridge Publishing

▶ **Use each fact family to write two addition and two subtraction number sentences.**

1.

2.

3.

__8__ + __5__ = __13__	___ + ___ = ___	___ + ___ = ___
___ + ___ = ___	___ + ___ = ___	___ + ___ = ___
___ − ___ = ___	___ − ___ = ___	___ − ___ = ___
___ − ___ = ___	___ − ___ = ___	___ − ___ = ___

Choose two different animals. Imagine how it would look if they were combined into one animal. Draw a picture of the new animal. Give it a name—for example, a monkey and a penguin could be called a *monguin*.

▶ **Write each word from the word bank under the word that has the same vowel sound.**

| coat | drove | fox | job |
| rock | rope | those | top |

nose   **pop**

_____   _____

_____   _____

_____   _____

_____   _____

You can make a secret code! Write all of the letters of the alphabet down one side of a piece of paper. Next to each letter, make a simple symbol such as a circle, star, happy face, heart, or plus sign. A computer keyboard is a good place to get ideas for symbols. Now, use the symbols to make words. Write a note with your new secret code.

▶ **Complete each table.**

1.

Subtract 5	
9	4
5	
7	
10	
11	
8	

2.

Subtract 3	
10	
9	
7	
8	
6	
11	

3.

Subtract 2	
11	
7	
9	
5	
8	
6	

You will need stairs and a ball to play this game. Stand at the bottom of the stairs and toss the ball toward the top, so the ball bounces down the stairs. Count the stairs the ball bounces on. Try to throw the ball so that it bounces on as many stairs as possible.

▶ **Say the name of each picture. Circle the letters that you hear in the word.**

1.

   ir   or   er

2.

   ur   or   ar

3.

   ir   or   ar

4.

   or   ur   ar

5.

   er   or   ar

6.

   ir   er   ar

 Make a marble obstacle course. Use boxes, toilet paper tubes, spools, and other small objects to make obstacles for a marble to go around, through, and over. Then, use a chopstick or wooden craft stick to push your marble through the course.

▶ **Use the mileage maps to answer the questions.**

1. How many miles is it from Salt Lake City to Bountiful?_____

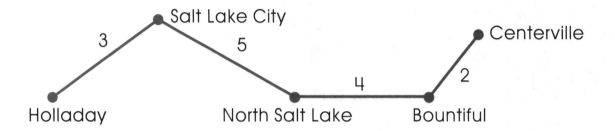

Salt Lake City

3   5

Holladay   North Salt Lake   Bountiful

4   2

Centerville

2. How many miles is it from Provo to Pleasant Grove?_____

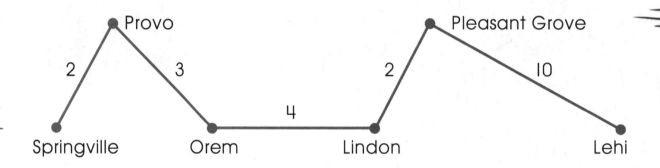

Provo   Pleasant Grove

2   3   2   10

Springville   Orem   Lindon   Lehi

4

How high can you stack rocks? Collect several flat rocks. See how tall you can stack them. You can use stacks of rocks as a natural way to mark a trail.

▶ Read each sentence. If the underlined word is spelled correctly, circle *yes*. If the underlined word is not spelled correctly, circle *no*.

1. Uma is a very <u>brav</u> girl.   yes   no

2. The United States flag is red, white, and <u>bloo</u>.   yes   no

3. Those girls were in my <u>class</u>.   yes   no

4. Gina is a very <u>helpfull</u> friend.   yes   no

5. I turned off the <u>light</u>.   yes   no

6. This glue is sticky <u>stuf</u>.   yes   no

7. Is <u>shee</u> coming with us?   yes   no

Write the name of a food for every letter of the alphabet. Circle your three favorites.

213

▶ **Add to find each sum.**

1. 24 + 12	**2.** 28 + 11	**3.** 32 + 26	**4.** 42 + 27

5. 75 + 24	**6.** 24 + 15	**7.** 81 + 14	**8.** 40 + 40

9. 18 20 + 11	**10.** 41 6 + 32	**11.** 66 22 + 11	**12.** 13 22 + 24

How strong is your breath? Get a variety of small, light objects, such as cotton balls, popped popcorn, table tennis balls, and feathers. Put them on a table and blow through a straw to move them with your breath. Which object is the easiest to move? Which is the hardest?

▶ **Circle *g* if the word begins like *game*. Circle *j* if the word begins like *gel*.**

1. giant

    g   j

2. giraffe

    g   j

3. goat

    g   j

4. gate

    g   j

5. golf

    g   j

6. gentle

    g   j

7. gym

    g   j

8. gem

    g   j

9. girl

    g   j

Get six to eight cups, bowls, and containers that look about the same size. Line them up starting with the one that you think will hold the least amount of water and ending with the one that you think will hold the most. Check your guess by using a measuring cup to fill each container with water.

► **Count the hundreds, tens, and ones. Write the number.**

1.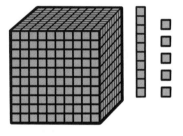

_____ hundreds, _____ tens,

and _____ ones = _____

2.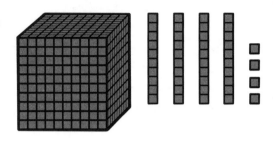

_____ hundred, _____ tens,

and _____ ones = _____

3.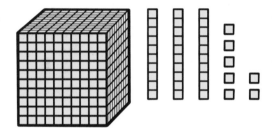

_____ hundred, _____ ten,

and _____ ones = _____

4.

_____ hundred, _____ tens,

and _____ ones = _____

Try writing a short note with the hand you do not normally write with. See if a friend or family member can read it.

▶ **Write one sentence for each meaning of the word** *bat*.

1. **bat:** a wooden stick that is used to hit a ball

_____

_____

_____

2. **bat:** a small animal that flies at night

_____

_____

_____

Find natural objects with interesting shapes, such as leaves, flowers, rocks, and shells. Trace the outlines of your shapes on a piece of white paper. Make your shapes overlap to create an interesting design. Color your design.

▶ **Circle the picture with the same beginning blend as the first picture.**

I.				
2.				
3.				

▶ **Write the word from the word bank that completes each sentence. Circle the beginning blend.**

sky	twins	stamp	snow

4. I need a _____ to mail my letter.

5. Jill and Bill are _____ .

6. Let's go sledding in the _____ .

7. Look at the clouds in the _____ .

Go outside and lie down on your side in the grass. Imagine what your life would be like if you were shorter than a blade of grass. Go back inside and write a story about what it would be like to be that small. Illustrate it.

218

▶ **Write the numeral for each number word.**

1. ninety-six _____   2. twenty-one _____

3. eighty-two _____   4. thirty-seven _____

5. sixty-five _____   6. sixty-one _____

7. seventy-nine _____   8. fifty-eight _____

9. twenty-two _____   10. eighty _____

11. eighteen _____   12. one hundred _____

13. twelve _____   14. twenty _____

15. forty-four _____   16. thirty-four _____

Stand in the middle of a room. Bend at your waist and touch your toes. Now, stand with your back against a wall. Try to touch your toes again. Can you do it?

▶ **Draw a line to match each phrase with the word it describes.**

1. The time of day when the sun goes down is   A. clock.

2. The place where dolphins live is the   B. bird.

3. Something near you is   C. babies.

4. A crow is a kind of   D. snail.

5. An object that tells time is a   E. close.

6. Apples are a kind of   F. sunset.

7. A small animal with a shell is a   G. ocean.

8. A shop is a kind of   H. first.

9. The winner comes in   I. store.

10. Chicks, ducklings, and fawns are animal   J. fruit.

How many objects in your house are bigger than you are? Take a walk around your house with a pencil and a piece of paper. Write down everything you see that is bigger than you. Count them and write the total.

▶ **Look at each ruler. Write the length of each object in inches.**

1.

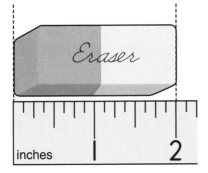

_____ in.

2.

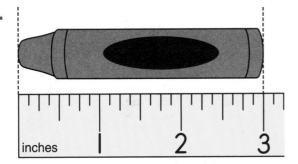

_____ in.

3.

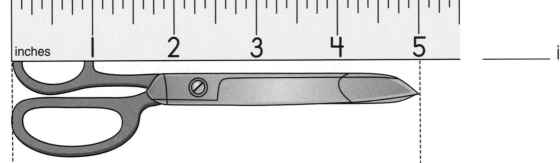

_____ in.

Try attracting butterflies with fruit. Butterflies like fruit that is a little overripe. You can take a soft peach, a mushy berry, or a banana that is turning brown and put it on a paper plate. Put the plate on a table, fencepost, or other platform. Watch for butterflies!

221

▶ **Write *was* or *were* to complete each sentence.**

1. Matt _____ excited.

2. The school play _____ about to start.

3. The play _____ about a toy maker.

4. Matt _____ the toy maker in the play.

5. Matt's parents _____ in the audience.

6. Many other parents _____ there too.

7. The teachers _____ sitting with their classes.

8. Matt _____ happy because he likes to act.

9. The curtains _____ beginning to open!

Put a penny on the ground. Try to bounce a tennis ball so that it hits the penny. Can you hit the penny in a way that makes it flip over?

▶ **Read the poem. Then, answer the questions.**

My Cat

Have you seen my cat?
Yes, I have seen your cat.

Really? My cat is big.
I saw a big cat.

My cat has spots.
I saw a big cat with spots.

My cat's spots are black.
I saw a big cat with black spots.

My cat runs fast.
I saw a big cat with black spots running fast.

You did see my cat! Where is it?
I do not know. I saw it last week.

1. What is the poem about? _____

2. Describe the cat. _____

_____

Hot weather can be hard on plants. Find a watering can or a plastic pitcher. Fill it with water. Walk around your yard and look for plants that might need a drink. Water them.

223

► **Color the shape whose number matches each description.**

1.

2 tens and 3 ones

2.

5 tens and 7 ones

3.

5 tens and 2 ones

4.

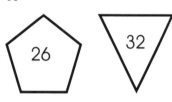

2 tens and 6 ones

5.

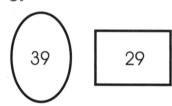

3 tens and 9 ones

6.

1 ten and 0 ones

Gather ten different sticks outside. First, put them in order starting with the shortest stick and ending with the longest. Then, put them in order starting with the thinnest stick and ending with the thickest stick. Finally, line them all up end to end and see how long they stretch.

224

▶ **Write each word from the word bank under the word that has the same vowel sound.**

blow	bowl	brown	clown	crown
elbow	how	mow	own	tower

cow   **pillow**

_____   _____

_____   _____

_____   _____

_____   _____

Make a boat out of aluminum foil. Float it in a big bowl full of water or in the sink. Now, add pennies to your boat. How many pennies can you add before it sinks?

▶ **Write the letter of each cause beside its effect.**

Effects	**Causes**
1. _____ Justin put on his hat and mittens.	A. It was cold outside.
2. _____ Chloe put ice in the water.	B. Her feet had grown.
3. _____ Ahmet gave his dog a bath.	C. The bike's tires were flat.
4. _____ Evan put air in his bike tires.	D. The rabbit was hungry.
5. _____ Kari got a new pair of shoes.	E. The water was warm.
6. _____ The rabbit ate the carrot.	F. The dog played in the mud.

Try eating your next meal using the hand you do not usually use to eat. Use that hand to hold your cup and eating utensils. Is it easy or hard?

▶ **Add the cost of the two items. Write the total in the box.**

1.

25¢   42¢

[ ]

2.

28¢   40¢

[ ]

3.

16¢   51¢

[ ]

4.

32¢   43¢

[ ]

You can make an ice cube necklace! Fill an ice cube tray with water. Lay a loop of yarn big enough to make a necklace over the tray. Push part of the yarn into each compartment, then carefully put the tray in the freezer. When the water is frozen, take your necklace out and wear it in the sun for a fun way to cool off.

▶ **Imagine that you are going on a trip. You can take only one thing. What would you take? Why?**

_____

_____

_____

_____

_____

_____

_____

_____

_____

Make a family of mice from rocks. Find three or four "mouse-shaped" rocks. Use glue to add string for the tails and small pieces of cloth or paper for the ears. Make the eyes, noses, and mouths with markers or paint.

► **Circle the correct rule for each number pattern.**

1.

2, 4, 6, 8, 10, 12

+2   +1

2.

20, 18, 16, 14, 12, 10

−2   −3

3.

50, 60, 70, 80, 90, 100

−10   +10

4.

80, 79, 78, 77, 76, 75

+10   −1

Make your name into a number. Look at the numbers and letters on a phone keypad and find the first letter of your name. Write down the number that is on that button. Do the same thing for all the letters in your name. Now, your name has its own phone number!

229

▶ **Say the name of each picture. Write the letters to complete each word.**

1.

so_____ _____

2.

_____ _____apes

3.

fi_____ _____

4.

_____ _____irt

5.

_____ _____ide

6.

ri_____ _____

Fill a clear glass halfway with water. Pour about half an inch of cooking oil into the glass. The oil will stay on top because oil is lighter than water. Add a few pinches of salt and watch what happens.

▶ **Read the passage. Then, answer the questions.**

Stamp Collecting

Are you a **philatelist**? If you collect stamps, that is what you are! Stamp collecting is a fun and interesting hobby.

If you want to start collecting stamps, you will need a few supplies. You will need a pair of tweezers to move the stamps so that they do not get dirty. You will also need an album with plastic pages to store your stamps.

Start by collecting some stamps. The stamps you collect can be new or used. You can collect stamps from letters that are delivered to your house. You can also buy stamps to add to your collection.

Next, decide how to sort your stamps. You can group them by their value, by the places they are from, or by the types of pictures on them. Then, place the stamps in your album.

Keep your stamp album in a cool, dry place away from direct sunlight. Heat, sun, and dampness can ruin your stamps.

1. Which sentence tells the main idea of the passage?

    A. Stamp collecting is a fun and interesting hobby.

    B. You can organize stamps in many different ways.

    C. Stamps come from all over the world.

2. What is a **philatelist**? _____

    _____

Cover your bedroom door in colorful construction paper. Use different colors and make a picture or a pattern.

▶ **Write a fraction that shows how much of each shape is colored.**

1.

2.

3.

Draw six large circles on a piece of paper. Label them with the words *angry, happy, sad, surprised, scared,* and *confused.* Draw faces in the circles to match each word.

▶ **Complete each sentence with the correct compound word from the word bank.**

cartwheel	sunflower
snowflakes	grandfather
fireworks	waterfall

1. The _____ lit up the night sky.

2. My mother's dad is my _____.

3. In gym class, we learned how to do a _____.

4. The _____ is a large, yellow flower.

5. When the first _____ fall, we know winter is coming.

6. We pitched our tent near a beautiful _____.

Collect about thirty small, pretty rocks. Glue them onto a heavy-duty paper plate in an interesting design.

233

► **Write a word from the word bank that makes sense in each sentence. Use each word only once.**

hop	bark	duck	roar	bird	fly

1. A _____ can swim.

2. Birds can _____ .

3. Lions can _____ .

4. Frogs can _____ .

5. Dogs can _____ .

6. A _____ can sing.

Snap, clap, stomp! How many sounds can you make with your body without using your voice? Try to make at least eight different noises.

▶ **Solve each problem. Circle the largest sum in each row.**

1. 6 + 5 = _____   0 + 9 = _____   7 + 8 = _____   8 + 9 = _____

2. 8 + 8 = _____   3 + 6 = _____   9 + 9 = _____   5 + 7 = _____

3. 6 + 3 = _____   5 + 5 = _____   9 + 4 = _____   7 + 9 = _____

4. 8 + 3 = _____   2 + 2 = _____   9 + 5 = _____   6 + 7 = _____

You can decorate the wheels of your bike by weaving party streamers through the spokes. Try using two different colors. Have a friend or family member watch you ride your bike. How do the wheels look?

▶ **Read the story. Circle each answer that might explain what is happening in the story. There may be more than one answer.**

What Is Missing?

Murphy's mom quickly pulled everything out of the dryer. Then, she lifted the lid of the washer, looked inside, and shook her head. She looked around the kitchen and family room, and then she rushed upstairs. "I cannot find it," she called to Murphy. "The last time I saw it was after the game on Saturday. We have to find it before 4:00!"

A. Murphy's mom has friends coming over at 4:00.

B. Murphy's mom is looking for Murphy's soccer jersey.

C. Murphy has a game today at 4:00.

D. Murphy's mom lost her purse.

It is important to be a good friend. Make a list of all the qualities a good friend should have. Circle the three most important qualities.

▶ **Use a metric ruler to measure each object. Write the length in centimeters.**

I.  _____ cm

2. _____ cm

 Choose an article from an old children's magazine. Guess how many times the word *and* is used in the article. Read the article and use a highlighter pen to highlight the word *and* whenever you see it. Count the highlights to see if your guess was correct.

237

► Follow the directions below to increase your endurance.

Build your endurance and have a hopping good time doing it! Grab a jump rope and find some happy music. Turn on the music and start jumping rope. See how long you can jump as you listen to your favorite songs. Rest in between songs based on your stamina. (Stamina just means your "staying power" or how long you can do something until you need a break.) If jumping rope is too difficult, you can still improve your endurance by jumping in place. In a few days, try again and see how many songs you can jump through. By the end of the summer, you may be able to jump through even more music, and your endurance will be better!

Make a mobile using objects you find in nature. Start by using string to tie two sticks together in the shape of a plus sign. Tie a string to the center of the plus sign for hanging your mobile when it is done. Use string to hang interesting natural objects, such as leaves, pinecones, and twigs to the sticks. Try to place the objects so that your mobile will hang evenly.

▶ **Circle the word that makes sense in the sentence.**

1. At night, the sky is _____ .

   green   dark   down

2. A frog got _____ in the pond.

   wet   when   hop

3. The _____ came to the party.

   game   sun   girls

4. A rabbit can _____ to the fence.

   hop   hat   boy

5. Mike took a trip on the _____ .

   swing   school   train

Put a small "treasure" such as a few coins, a toy, or a pretty shell in a plastic container. Hide your treasure somewhere in your yard. Make a map of your yard that shows how to find your treasure. Draw an "X" to mark the spot where your treasure is!

▶ **Use the chart to answer each question.**

Allowance for Each Chore Completed	
Bundle newspapers for recycling	$0.25
Empty wastepaper baskets	$0.75
Put away groceries	$0.50
Wash the car	$2.00
Set the table	$1.00

1. Which chore pays the most money? _____

2. Which chore pays the least money? _____

3. If Hugo sets the table for dinner every night this week, how much

   will he earn? _____

4. Davis bundled newspapers for recycling two times this week.

   How much money did he earn? _____

Tape a piece of paper to the floor near a wall. Put a pencil between your first and second toes and try to write your name. Lean on the wall for balance.

▶ **Read each statement. Write Y for yes or N for no beside each statement.**

How a Snake Is Like a Turtle

How a Bike Is Like a Truck

1. _____ Both have shells.

2. _____ Both can be on land.

3. _____ Both are reptiles.

4. _____ Both have scales.

5. _____ Both have tires.

6. _____ Both need gas.

7. _____ Both can be new.

8. _____ Both have four wheels.

Compound words are made from two small words put together to make one big word. Look around your house and yard for compound words. For example, you might walk through a *doorway* and see a *lampshade* next to an *armchair*. Write down all of the compound words that you find.

▶ **Color each shape to show the fraction.**

1.

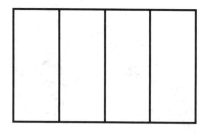

$$\frac{3}{4}$$

2.

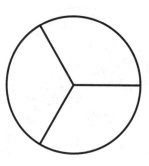

$$\frac{1}{3}$$

3.

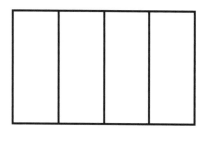

$$\frac{1}{4}$$

4.

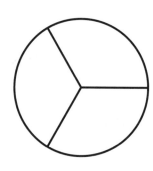

$$\frac{2}{3}$$

Ask an adult for envelopes from his or her junk mail. Look at the return address on one of the envelopes and find out what state the letter was mailed from. See if you can find that state on a map.

242

▶ **Write each word from the word bank under the word that has the same beginning sound.**

cake	camp	candy	center	cereal
circle	city	coat	corn	cent

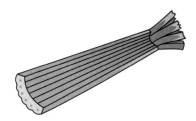

celery

cat

_____   _____

_____   _____

_____   _____

_____   _____

Make fifteen dots on a piece of paper in no particular order. Look at your dots and see if you can connect them to make a picture. If you do not have any ideas, try turning the paper sideways or upside down.

▶ **Solve each word problem.**

1. There are 26 students on one bus. There are 29 students on the other bus. How many students are on the buses altogether?

2. Cynthia found 47 shells on the beach. Byron found 44 shells on the beach. How many shells did they find in all?

3. Tony ran 15 laps on Monday. He ran 17 laps on Tuesday. How many laps did Tony run altogether?

4. Thomas saw 48 fish in one fish tank. Brooke saw 36 fish in another fish tank. How many fish did they see in all?

Guess how many very big steps it would take you to cross your yard. Walk across your yard using very big steps and counting them to check your guess. Now, try the same thing with very small steps.

▶ **Write sentences with the correct punctuation.**

1. Write a sentence that ends with a period (.).

_____

_____

2. Write a sentence that ends with a question mark (?).

_____

_____

3. Write a sentence that ends with an exclamation point (!).

_____

_____

Tape a strong magnet to the center of a small paper plate. Turn the plate upside down on a table. Use paperclips, washers, or bolts to build a magnetic sculpture on top of the plate.

245

▶ **Use each fact family to write two addition and two subtraction number sentences.**

1. Family: 6, 7, 13

_____ + _____ = _____

_____ + _____ = _____

_____ − _____ = _____

_____ − _____ = _____

2. Family: 7, 8, 15

_____ + _____ = _____

_____ + _____ = _____

_____ − _____ = _____

_____ − _____ = _____

3. Family: 6, 8, 14

_____ + _____ = _____

_____ + _____ = _____

_____ − _____ = _____

_____ − _____ = _____

4. Family: 7, 5, 12

_____ + _____ = _____

_____ + _____ = _____

_____ − _____ = _____

_____ − _____ = _____

Write the numbers 1 to 9 on nine different index cards. Mix them up with the number sides down, then draw three cards. Use them to make the biggest number you can. For example, the digits 3, 9, and 6 would make the number 963. Put the cards back and try it again.

▶ **How many sentences can you write using only the words in the word bank? Write the sentences below.**

and	at	barks	bed	big	blue	boy
car	Dad	dog	girl	I	it	little
Mom	over	parks	ran	red	small	squirrel
the	to	tree	under	up	walks	yellow

_____

_____

_____

_____

_____

_____

_____

_____

Try this with a friend. Start by standing across from each other, then turn around so you are facing away from each other. Now, each of you should change one small thing about yourself. For example, you could untuck your shirt, untie one shoe, take out a hair clip, or roll up your sleeves. When you are both ready, turn around and try to guess what each of you has changed.

247

► **Use the calendars to answer each question.**

May						
S	M	T	W	Th	F	S
			1	2	3	4
5	6	7	8	9	10	11
12	13	14	15	16	17	18
19	20	21	22	23	24	25
26	27	28	29	30	31	

June						
S	M	T	W	Th	F	S
						1
2	3	4	5	6	7	8
9	10	11	12	13	14	15
16	17	18	19	20	21	22
23	24	25	26	27	28	29
30						

1. Julia went to the dentist on the third Tuesday in May. What was the date?

Tuesday, May _____

2. Heath started his dance class on the first Monday in June. What was the date?

Monday, June _____

3. Today is May 10. Adam's family will see a play next Thursday. On what date will they see a play?

Thursday, May _____

4. How many days are between May 29 and June 5?

_____

Before you start eating a bowl of ice cream, oatmeal, or soup, guess how many spoonfuls it will take for you to eat the whole bowl. Count your spoonfuls as you eat to see if your guess was correct.

▶ **Draw a line to match the words that rhyme.**

1. cat   ten

2. but   big

3. pig   fog

4. hen   rut

5. log   hat

6. cake   jeep

7. rice   rake

8. sheep   cone

9. bone   flute

10. chute   mice

Make a list of ten good things that have happened to you in the last week. Share your list with a friend or family member.

► **What do you think is the most difficult part about being a parent?**

_____

_____

_____

_____

_____

_____

_____

_____

_____

Go on a button quest! See how many buttons you can find. Check at crosswalks or in the window of your family car. You may even find a button near your front door.

▶ **Read the poem. Then, draw a line to match each sense with a detail in the poem.**

Pitter-Patter

Pitter-patter, pitter-patter.
How I love the rain!

Storm clouds moving in,
The rain is about to begin.
How I love to see the rain!

Tiny sprinkles on my face,
Little droplets playing chase.
How I love to feel the rain!

I open up my mouth so wide,
Letting little drops inside.
How I love to taste the rain!

Tapping on my window,
It's a rhythm that I know.
How I love to hear the rain!

Everything looks so green,
And the fresh air smells so clean.
How I love to smell the rain!

Pitter-patter, pitter-patter.
How I love the rain!

	Sense	Detail
1.	sight	tapping a rhythm on the window
2.	touch	storm clouds moving in
3.	taste	little drops inside my mouth
4.	hearing	tiny sprinkles on my face
5.	smell	clean, fresh air

Stretch a rope across your yard. Try to walk along the rope backward.

▶ **Write how many tens and ones.**

1. 12 is the same as _____ ten and _____ ones.

2. 93 is the same as _____ tens and _____ ones.

3. 44 is the same as _____ tens and _____ ones.

4. 76 is the same as _____ tens and _____ ones.

5. 81 is the same as _____ tens and _____ one.

6. 55 is the same as _____ tens and _____ ones.

7. 39 is the same as _____ tens and _____ ones.

8. 60 is the same as _____ tens and _____ ones.

Plan a letter meal. Choose a letter and make a lunch that contains only items that begin with that letter. For example, if you chose the letter *C*, you could have chicken strips, carrots, corn, and a chocolate chip cookie for dessert.

▶ An analogy is a way to show how things are alike. To complete an analogy, look at the first set of words. Decide how they are related. Apply that relationship to the second set of words.

> Finger : hand :: toe : **foot**
>
> A finger is part of a hand. A toe is part of a foot.

▶ Use the words from the word bank to complete each analogy.

> light   sky   square   table

1. sleep : bed :: eat : _____

2. three : triangle :: four : _____

3. green : grass :: blue : _____

4. win : lose :: dark : _____

Here is a fun way to decorate your bike helmet. Cut party streamers into four or five strips. The strips should be about half as long as your arm. Tape the strips to the back of your helmet. When you ride your bike fast, the streamers will fly out behind you!

▶ **Solve each problem.**

EXAMPLE:
Nick left for school on the bus at 8:00.
The bus ride took 20 minutes.   Think: 8:00 + 0:20 = 8:20
What time did Nick get to school?

1. Claire ate a snack at 10:00. She ate lunch 2 hours later. What time did she eat lunch?

_____

2. This morning, Hau read for 15 minutes. He started at 9:00. What time did he finish reading?

_____

3. Recess lasted 30 minutes. It started at 2:00. What time did it end?

_____

4. Ellis left school at 3:30. He rode the bus for 30 minutes. What time did he get off of the bus?

_____

Pick out three pairs of shorts and three shirts. Lay one shirt and one pair of shorts on your bed. That is one outfit. How many different outfits can you make using just those six pieces of clothing?

▶ **Say each word aloud. Write the syllables in the boxes.**

1. apartment ☐ ☐☐☐☐ ☐☐☐☐

2. enormous ☐ ☐☐☐ ☐☐☐☐

3. subtraction ☐☐☐ ☐☐☐☐ ☐☐☐☐

4. wonderful ☐☐☐ ☐☐☐ ☐☐☐

5. adventure ☐☐ ☐☐☐ ☐☐☐☐

How many dots do you think there are on a die that you use for playing games? Do the math problem in your head or on paper. Then, count the dots to see if you are right.

▶ **Add to find each sum. Use the number line to help you add hundreds.**

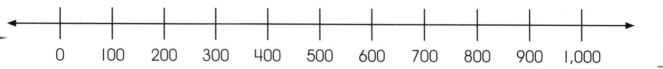

0   100   200   300   400   500   600   700   800   900   1,000

1. 300 + 200 = _____

2. 700 + 200 = _____

3. 100 + 200 = _____

4. 600 + 400 = _____

5. 400 + 400 = _____

6. 500 + 200 = _____

7. 100 + 500 = _____

8. 400 + 500 = _____

Get 26 index cards and write each of the letters of the alphabet on a card. Mix up the cards, letter side down, and pick six of them. Try to use some of the letters you picked to form a word that is at least three letters long. Put the letters you did not use back with the unused cards, then mix them up again and pick six more cards. Keep going until you cannot form any more words.

► **Read the table of contents. Write the chapter and page number where you should begin looking for the answer to each question.**

Table of Contents

1. How long do lions live? Chapter _____ Page _____

2. How fast do sailfish swim? Chapter _____ Page _____

3. What color is a robin's egg? Chapter _____ Page _____

4. Do spiders bite? Chapter _____ Page _____

5. What is the difference between frogs and toads?

   Chapter _____ Page _____

Use cooked spaghetti noodles to make the letters of your name. Leave them on a flat surface to dry. When they are hard, you can glue them in order onto a dark piece of paper.

▶ **Read the story. Then, fill in the table.**

Rachel's Birthday

Today is Rachel's birthday. She invited four friends to her party. Each friend brought a gift. Rachel's brother mixed up the tags on the gifts. Can you use the clues to put the tags on the correct gifts?

Grace's gift has flowered wrapping paper and a bow.

Kate's gift is small and has a bow.

Meghan forgot to put a bow on her gift.

Jade's gift has striped wrapping paper.

▶ **Write O in the box when you know a gift was brought by the girl. Write X in the box when you know a gift was not brought by the girl.**

Kate				
Grace				
Jade				
Meghan				

Collect ten similar small stones, ten similar small twigs, and ten small pinecones or acorns. Use your natural objects to make a pattern on the ground. Then, use them to make an interesting design.

▶ **If you could give any gift in the world, what would you give? Whom would you give the gift to? Write your answers below.**

_____

_____

_____

_____

_____

_____

_____

_____

_____

How many seeds are in an orange? Find out by peeling an orange and dividing it into sections. Take the seeds out as you find them and put them on a plate. Count the seeds and then eat the orange!

▶ **Read the story. Then, read the directions that follow.**

Aunt Antonym

We have a nickname for my mother's sister. We call her Aunt Antonym. She always says or does the opposite of what we say or do. One day, we all went to the zoo. At the monkey exhibit, we thought the monkeys were cute. My aunt thought that they were strange. Soon, we were hungry. My aunt was still full from breakfast. After lunch, we rode the train around the zoo. My aunt wanted to walk. Finally, my aunt said that she was tired and ready to go. We were still full of energy. We wished we could have stayed.

▶ **Write _T_ next to each statement that is true. Write _F_ next to each statement that is false.**

1. _____ The author is writing about his sister.

2. _____ Aunt Antonym is the real name of the author's aunt.

3. _____ Aunt Antonym was full from breakfast.

4. _____ Aunt Antonym did not want to ride the train.

▶ **Write a word from the story that is an antonym for each word.**

5. ride_____   6. stay _____

7. energetic _____   8. hungry_____

Fill a beach pail with water. Put a quarter at the bottom, in the center. Now, try to drop a penny so it lands exactly on the quarter.

▶ **Follow the directions to solve each problem.**

1. Start with 800.
   Write the number that is 200 less. _____

2. Start with 600.
   Write the number that is 300 less. _____

3. Start with 200.
   Write the number that is 100 less. _____

4. Start with 700.
   Write the number that is 500 less. _____

5. Start with 900.
   Write the number that is 400 less. _____

6. Start with 600.
   Write the number that is 100 less. _____

7. Start with 500.
   Write the number that is 500 less. _____

Use a permanent pen to write the numbers 1 to 9 all over a beach ball. You will need to use each number several times. Throw the ball in the air and catch it. Add the two numbers that are under your hands when you catch the ball. You can play this game by yourself or with a friend.

► **Follow the directions below to create a Loyalty List.**

How can you show your loyalty this summer? Being loyal means supporting and standing up for those you love. What can you do to practice this important trait? Try making a Loyalty List. Ask an adult for a large sheet of poster board and markers. Write the things that you will do to show loyalty to those you love, such as your family and friends. Then, decorate the poster board with pictures of your friends and family. With the adult's permission, place the poster on the wall or door in your bedroom. It will help you remember how you can be loyal every day. After a week, look at your Loyalty List and write examples of how you have shown your loyalty.

Write your name in the middle of a piece of white drawing paper. Choose a color you like and draw an outline around your name. Choose another color and draw around the outline. Keep going with different colors until you reach the edge of the page.

Write *person*, *place*, or *thing* after each sentence to identify the highlighted noun.

1. The children left **school** early today. _____

2. They went to the **park** to play soccer. _____

3. The **teacher** watched the children play. _____

4. A **squirrel** climbed the tree. _____

5. The boys and girls rowed a **boat**. _____

6. One **girl** went down the slide. _____

7. The **boy** was feeding the ducks. _____

8. Two girls were walking their **dog**. _____

Go on a pattern hunt. Walk around your house looking for different patterns. Some places you might find patterns include clothing, wallpaper, paper towels, floor and counter tiles, furniture coverings, table cloths, and placemats. Make a tally mark on a piece of paper for every pattern you see.

263

► **Complete each number pattern. Write the rule.**

1. 2, 4, 6, 8,_____ ,_____ ,_____ ,_____ ,_____ ,_____

Rule: _____

2. 10, 20, 30,_____ ,_____ ,_____ ,_____ ,_____ ,_____

Rule: _____

3. 5, 10, 15,_____ ,_____ ,_____ ,_____ ,_____ ,_____

Rule: _____

4. 3, 6, 9, 12,_____ ,_____ ,_____ ,_____ ,_____ ,_____

Rule: _____

Here is a fun way to give someone a secret note. First, write your note on a small piece of paper and fold it up. Then, wrap yarn around your note until it is in the center of a small ball. Give the ball of yarn to the person you want to receive the note and see if he or she can find it!

▶ **Pretend that you are planning a Silly Saturday party. Write a letter to invite someone to your party.**

Dear _____,

_____

_____

_____

_____

_____

_____

_____

Your friend,

_____

Think of a fun nickname for yourself and everyone in your family. Make nametags for everyone to wear. Call each other by your new names for the rest of the day.

► **Repeated addition problems help you get ready for multiplication. Add to find each sum.**

1.	3	2.	2	3.	4	4.	5
	3		2		4		5
	+ 3		+ 2		+ 4		+ 5

5.	3	6.	2	7.	5	8.	4
	3		2		5		4
	3		2		5		4
	+ 3		+ 2		+ 5		+ 4

 Here is something fun you can do with socks that do not have matches. Look at the biggest sock and guess how many of the other socks you can stuff inside it. Stuff the other socks in the big one to check your guess. Pack them tightly to get as many socks inside as you can.

266

▶ **Write each noun in the correct column.**

aunt	dad	France
cousin	restaurant	chair
lamp	bedroom	girl
basement	dresser	sink

Nouns for People   **Nouns for Places**   **Nouns for Things**

_____ _____ _____

_____ _____ _____

_____ _____ _____

_____ _____ _____

Write the letters of the alphabet down the left side of a piece of paper. For each letter, write a three-word sentence. Every word in the sentence must begin with that letter. For example, for "A," you could write "Ana ate apples" or "Apes are awesome."

267

► **Write the expanded form for each number.**

EXAMPLE:

251 = __2__ hundreds + __5__ tens + __I__ one = **200** + **50** + __I__

1. 341 = ____ hundreds + ____ tens + ____ one = ____ + ____ + ____

2. 563 = ____ hundreds + ____ tens + ____ ones = ____ + ____ + ____

3. 752 = ____ hundreds + ____ tens + ____ ones = ____ + ____ + ____

4. 845 = ____ hundreds + ____ tens + ____ ones = ____ + ____ + ____

5. 429 = ____ hundreds + ____ tens + ____ ones = ____ + ____ + ____

6. 684 = ____ hundreds + ____ tens + ____ ones = ____ + ____ + ____

Some flowers always have the same number of petals, while others can have different numbers. Find a group of the same type of flower. Count the petals on several different flowers. If the numbers are different, can you spot a pattern?

▶ **Write *a* or *an* in front of each noun.**

1. _____ lawyer

2. _____ mayor

3. _____ drummer

4. _____ officer

5. _____ author

6. _____ doctor

7. _____ diver

8. _____ scientist

9. _____ owner

10. _____ athlete

11. _____ clown

12. _____ explorer

13. _____ teacher

14. _____ artist

Make many tiny bubbles with straws. Get seven or eight plastic drinking straws and hold them all in one hand so the ends are even. Wrap tape around the straws so they stay together in a bundle. Dip one end of the bundle into a container of bubble liquid. Take the bundle out and blow through the other end.

▶ **Read the passage. Then, answer the questions.**

How Plants Grow

A plant needs energy to grow. Energy comes from food. A plant makes its food in its leaves. Sunlight and water help the plant make food. After you plant a seed, a tiny seedling pushes its way out from the soil. The plant grows toward the sun. The plant must get water, or it will dry out and die. The roots of the plant pull water and nutrients from the soil. If there is little rain where you live, you may need to water your plant. If the soil in your area has few nutrients, you may need to add plant food to the soil. That way your plant gets what it needs.

1. What is the main idea of this passage?

   A. A plant can die without water.

   B. Plants need food, water, and sunlight to grow.

   C. Plants start as seeds.

2. What happens after you plant a seed?_____

_____

Use twigs to form the letters of your name. Glue them together. When they are dry, you can hang them on your wall or glue them to a piece of paper.

▶ **Write a word problem for each number sentence.**

EXAMPLE:

3 + 2 = 5 I had 3 purple markers. My friend gave me 2 more.

Now, I have 5 purple markers.

1. 4 + 2 = 6 _____

_____

_____

2. 5 – 4 = 1 _____

_____

_____

Go on a leaf opposite hunt. First, find a leaf. Think of one word to describe your leaf. Then find a leaf that you could describe with the opposite word. Some words you could use for describing leaves include the following: *big* and *small*, *shiny* and *dull*, *smooth* and *rough*, *rounded* and *pointy*, *dark* and *light*.

271

▶ **Circle the adjective that describes each underlined noun.**

1. Insects have six <u>legs</u>.

2. Bumblebees have hairy <u>bodies</u>.

3. A beetle has a hard <u>body</u>.

4. Ladybugs have black <u>spots</u>.

5. Butterflies can be beautiful <u>colors</u>.

6. Termites have powerful <u>jaws</u>.

7. Dragonflies have four <u>wings</u>.

8. A green <u>grasshopper</u> jumps away.

Can you keep three balloons in the air at the same time? Use big, round balloons. Keep them floating by batting them into the air before they touch the ground. You can use a timer to see how long you can keep the balloons floating before one of them touches the ground.

Circle each sentence that is in the correct order and makes sense.

1. The most common pets are cats and dogs.

    Common dogs and cats are the most pets.

2. A pet needs food, exercise, and a good place to live.

    A good place to live needs food, exercise, and pets.

3. Love pet your is the best thing you give can.

    The best thing you can give your pet is love.

Sit on the floor with your legs crossed. Put your hands on your head. Now, try to stand up without letting any parts of your hands or arms touch the floor.

► **Follow the directions below to build endurance.**

One of the best ways to build endurance is to walk. Grab some friends or family members and get going! Find a safe place, such as a park path, school track, or nature trail. Choose a date and invite your loved ones to join you for a wacky walkathon. To make it fun, have everyone arrive wearing a costume or funny face paint. Then, get your silly group walking. Remind them that they can have fun but that they must walk fast because they are exercising! Some people may not be able to walk for as long or as fast as everyone else. That is OK as long as each walker is doing his best. Try to get the group to meet for several walkathons to get fitter and sillier as summer goes on!

Make a list of books that you have read. Next to each book, draw one to five stars. One star means you did not like the book very much. Five stars means that you loved it. Add to your list every time you read a new book.

Write each missing addend.

I. 9
  +☐
  13

2. 6
  +☐
  15

3. 9
  ☐+
  18

4. 4
  ☐+
  13

5. 4
  ☐+
  10

6. 7
  ☐+
  16

7. 7
  ☐+
  11

8. 6
  ☐+
  14

9. 8
  ☐+
  17

10. 8
  ☐+
  12

II. 5
  ☐+
  11

12. 9
  ☐+
  18

 See if you can find words on some of your toys or games that tell you where they were made. Then, try to find that country on a map or globe.

275

▶ **Read the story. Then, decide whether each sentence below is a fact or an opinion. Write F for fact or O for opinion.**

Winter Fun

Some people like spring, but I do not. I think that winter is the best season. My family goes to the mountains every year. My stepmom is a good skier. She skis while we watch. My dad wears snowshoes and goes on long walks. My brothers and I like to play in the snow. The nights are too cold to be outside. So, we stay warm in our cabin. My stepmom makes us hot chocolate at bedtime, and we tell stories.

1. _____ Winter is the best season.

2. _____ My family goes to the mountains.

3. _____ My stepmom makes us hot chocolate.

4. _____ I think my stepmom is a good skier.

5. _____ The nights are too cold.

6. _____ Dad goes on long walks.

How many legs are in your house? Remember, people are not the only ones that have legs. Animals, tables, and chairs all have legs too!

276

▶ **Read the passage. Then, answer the questions.**

The Moon

The moon lights up the night sky. Sometimes, the moon looks narrow. Sometimes, it looks round. The appearance of the moon has to do with the position of the moon as viewed from Earth. When the moon is between the sun and Earth, the moon looks black. This is called a new moon. When Earth is between the sun and the moon, the moon looks bright and round. This is called a full moon. In the middle of these periods, half of the moon is lit, and half of the moon is dark. It takes about one month for the moon to finish the entire cycle.

I.   What is the main idea of this passage?

     A.   The moon can look thin or fat.

     B.   The moon travels around Earth.

     C.   The moon looks different throughout the month.

2.   What makes the moon's appearance change? _____

     _____

3.   When does a full moon happen? _____

     _____

Write a sentence with exactly three words. Then, write a new sentence with exactly four words. Next, write a new sentence with exactly five words. Keep going, each time making the new sentence one word longer than the last one.

277

▶ **Circle the two bugs in each box with equal differences.**

1.

 7 – 2

 7 – 5

 5 – 3

2.

 9 – 8

 5 – 2

 4 – 3

3.

4 – 1

 7 – 2

 5 – 0

4.

6 – 6

9 – 9

4 – 2

Fold a piece of paper in half. On one side of the paper, draw a simple picture. Then, try to draw the same picture upside down on the other side of the paper.

▶ **Read the story. Then, decide whether each sentence below is a fact or an opinion. Write F for fact or O for opinion.**

Learning to Cook

My brother is helping me learn to cook. I think he is an excellent cook. Last night, we made noodles with tomato sauce. We also made spinach bread. We planned to bake a pie, but we ran out of flour. Mom loved the meal. She said, "You're hired!"

1. _____ I think my brother is an excellent cook.

2. _____ We ran out of flour.

3. _____ We made spinach bread.

4. _____ Pie is good.

Do you have a jigsaw puzzle that is too easy? You can make it harder by flipping over all the pieces so that you cannot see the pictures. Try putting the puzzle together with the pictures facing down.

▶ **Write and solve six addition problems. The answers should be between 11 and 18.**

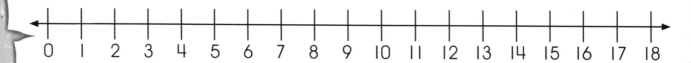

1. _____ + _____ = _____   2. _____ + _____ = _____

3. _____ + _____ = _____   4. _____ + _____ = _____

5. _____ + _____ = _____   6. _____ + _____ = _____

Use an inkpad to make your fingerprints on a piece of white paper. Use a magnifying glass to examine your fingerprints. How are they alike? How are they different?

▶ **Read the passage. Then, answer the questions.**

Teeth

Teeth are important for chewing food, so you need to take care of your teeth. When you are a child, you have baby teeth. These fall out and are replaced by adult teeth. You can expect to have 32 teeth one day. You should brush your teeth at least twice a day—once in the morning and once at bedtime. Also, you should floss to remove food that gets stuck between your teeth. That way, you will have a healthy smile!

1. What is the main idea of this passage?

    A. You can have a healthy smile.

    B. It is important to take care of your teeth.

    C. Adults have more teeth than children.

2. Why should you take care of your teeth? _____

    _____

3. What happens to baby teeth? _____

    _____

4. How many teeth do adults have? _____

You get three points for each piece of clothing you are wearing and four points for each of your shoes. Add up your outfit. How many points did you get?

▶ **Subtract to find each difference.**

1. 63
   − 40

2. 80
   − 60

3. 75
   − 50

4. 79
   − 20

5. 38
   − 10

6. 93
   − 30

7. 67
   − 40

8. 83
   − 20

9. 77
   − 10

10. 76
    − 50

11. 59
    − 30

12. 77
    − 60

Borrow the spoons, forks, and butter knives from the kitchen. On the table, make them into an interesting pattern. Record your pattern by drawing it on paper.

▶ **Write *to*, *too*, or *two* to finish each sentence.**

1. Are you checking out _____ books?

2. Is your birthday today, _____?

3. Amber is going _____ the ballet tonight.

4. The muffins are _____ hot to eat right now.

5. Please hand those _____ Becca.

6. I am riding my bike _____ the park.

7. That shirt was small, so I gave it _____ Paul.

8. My brother will be _____ years old on Friday.

Take out two different board games. Use the board from one of the games and the pieces from the other to invent a new game. Play it with your family.

283

▶ **Tara and her dad planted a tiny pine tree in their yard on her sixth birthday. They measured it every year on her birthday to see how many inches it had grown. Look at the graph and answer the questions.**

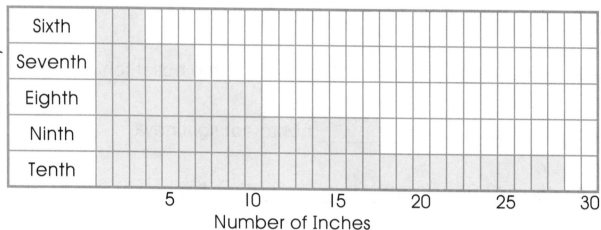

Growth of Tara's Pine Tree

1. How tall was the tree when Tara planted it? _____

2. How tall was the tree on Tara's eighth birthday? _____

3. On which birthday was the tree 17 inches tall? _____

4. How many inches did the tree grow from Tara's seventh

   birthday to her ninth birthday? _____

See if you can figure out when your half birthday is. Your half birthday is exactly six months after your real birthday. Mark your half birthday on your family's calendar.

▶ **Decide if each word is a noun or a verb. Write** *noun* **or** *verb* **on the line.**

1. horse _____

2. run _____

3. baker _____

4. tree _____

5. car _____

6. boy _____

7. lawn _____

8. see _____

9. grow _____

10. barn _____

Make a list of twenty toys or games that do not need batteries and do not have electrical plugs. Circle the three toys or games that you like best.

285

Circle the number sentences that are true.

1. $7 = 7$

2. $8 > 5$

3. $7 = 8$

4. $9 < 7$

5. $4 + 3 = 7$

6. $6 = 4 + 3$

7. $2 + 3 = 5$

8. $2 = 1 + 1$

9. $7 + 4 = 3$

10. $9 = 3 + 6$

11. $5 + 2 = 5 + 2$

12. $4 + 3 = 3 + 4$

13. $4 + 6 = 5 + 3$

14. $5 + 6 = 10$

Cut a piece of paper the same size as a dollar bill. Pretend that you get to design a new dollar. Draw your new dollar on the paper. Remember to use both sides, just like a real dollar bill.

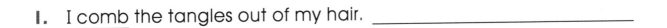

▶ **Which part of speech is underlined in each sentence? Write** *noun*, *verb*, **or** *adjective*.

1. I <u>comb</u> the tangles out of my hair. _____

2. Riley has a red <u>comb</u>. _____

3. Cassidy likes <u>cherry</u> pie. _____

4. I want to eat that <u>cherry</u>. _____

5. The fruit <u>bat</u> hangs upside down to sleep. _____

6. Felipe and Joe <u>bat</u> the ball over the fence. _____

7. Turn on the <u>light</u>. _____

8. Gerry carried the <u>light</u> bag. _____

Old greeting cards can make nice bookmarks. Just cut the picture on the front of the card into a bookmark-sized strip. Decorate the back with your own design.

▶ Can you use salt and a piece of string to "catch" an ice cube?

Materials:
- ice cube
- salt
- string

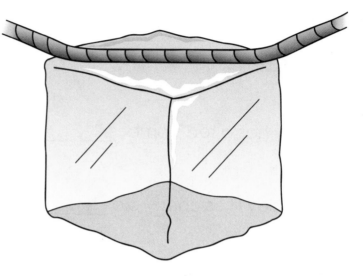

Procedure:

1. Try to catch the ice cube with the piece of string. (You cannot tie the string around the ice cube.) Can you do it?

2. Next, place the string on the ice cube and sprinkle a little salt on the string. Count to 30 and slowly lift the string. The ice cube will be attached!

What Is This All About?

When you sprinkle salt on the ice, it lowers the freezing temperature of the ice. This causes some water to melt around the string. When the water forms, it dilutes the salt on the ice and allows the water to freeze around the string. This is why you can pick it up.

For five or ten minutes, do everything in slow motion. Walk slowly. Eat slowly. Be sure to talk to someone during that time and to talk very slowly.

▶ **Complete each sentence with a helping verb from the word bank.**

are	can	have	is

1. Sue _____ tie her shoes.

2. I _____ cleaned my room.

3. We _____ going to the store.

4. Mrs. Vasquez _____ helping us.

▶ **Underline the helping verb in each sentence. Circle the verb that comes after the helping verb.**

5. Shonda was calling your name.

6. I am going to the movies.

7. We are playing in the rain.

8. They were running home.

9. Peter might go to the pool today.

10. We could eat our dinner.

How many months old were you on your last birthday? Remember, there are twelve months in every year. You may need a pencil and paper to figure this out.

▶ **Draw a line to match each number word to the correct numeral.**

1. twenty-three   99

    seventy-five   11

    sixty-two   23

    ninety-nine   32

    eighteen   18

    thirty-two   62

    eleven   75

2. fifteen   100

    eighty-four   84

    forty-seven   12

    twenty-six   15

    fifty-three   47

    twelve   53

    one hundred   26

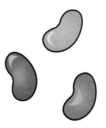

Start a list of things that make you happy. Try to put at least ten things on your list. Put the list on your refrigerator and ask other people in your family to add to the list with things that make them happy. If the page gets full, tape another page to the bottom.

▶ **Can you hold two streams of water together? Or, can you separate two streams of water that had been flowing together? You would probably have to be pretty powerful! Or would you?**

Materials:
- nail (8- or 16-penny)
- water
- hammer
- masking tape
- soup can (empty)

Procedure:

1. Ask an adult to use a hammer and nail to make two small holes in the lower section of the soup can. The holes should be close to the bottom and 0.5 inches (1.27 cm) apart. Tape over the holes.

2. Fill the can with water and hold it over a sink. Then, remove the tape.

3. Using your fingers, try to pinch the two streams of water together.

4. Using your fingers, try to split the two streams of water.

What Is This All About?

When you pinch the streams of water together, the water molecules act like magnets. They attract each other and form larger water drops.

By splitting the water streams, you push the streams far enough away that they cannot attract each other. So, they stay separate. As long as you have water in the can, you will be able to pinch or split the streams of water.

Draw five pictures. The first one should be of a tadpole and the last one should be of a frog. The three pictures in the middle should show how the tadpole turns into a frog.

▶ **Follow the directions below to create your own desert dessert.**

A relief map shows the physical features of a place, such as rivers and mountains. Sometimes it is called a topographical map. You will call this a delicious map when you are finished with this activity!

Make this map in the kitchen with an adult's help. You will need two packages of prepared sugar cookie dough. You will also need some toppings, such as chocolate syrup, sliced fruit, and sprinkles.

Press the cookie dough from one package onto a cookie sheet. Use the other package of cookie dough to mold and shape land features. You could make mountains, hills, islands, volcanoes, deserts, forests, and valleys.

Bake the "map," following the directions on the package. Let the map cool. Use chocolate syrup to make water features, such as lakes and rivers. Highlight other features with different toppings.

Share the dessert with your family. Tell them what you learned about relief maps.

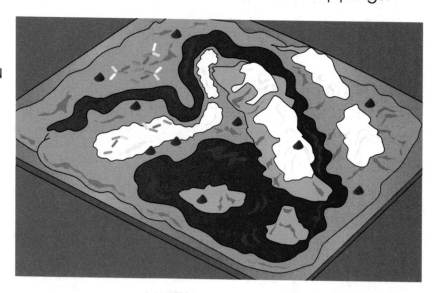

Get four index cards. On each card, draw lines to show how you could cut the card into four equal pieces. Try to draw a different way on each card.

▶ **Read the story. Then, match the question with the correct answer.**

A Walk in the Woods

One cold, winter day Missy and Kim went for a walk in the woods. They saw a deer eating the bark of a tree. When Kim stepped on a twig, the deer suddenly ran away. The girls decided it was too cold to keep walking. They went home.

1. Who went for a walk?   the woods

2. What season was it?   Missy and Kim

3. What did the deer eat?   It was too cold.

4. Where did the girls go for a walk?   winter

5. Why did the girls go home?   the bark of a tree

Here is a fun surprise you can make for an adult. Cut out eight small squares of paper the same size as the keys on the adult's computer keyboard. Write the eight letters *I,L,O,V,E,Y,O,* and *U* on the eight squares. Use double-sided tape or tape loops to stick the squares to keys on the keyboard to form the words *I LOVE YOU.*

▶ Follow the directions below to learn more about animals.

Studying animals is a great way to learn about different places in the world. Go to the library and check out books about animals that live in other parts of the world. Or, search the Internet with an adult to find out about animals. Choose an animal that lives on each continent (Africa, Antarctica, Asia, Australia, Europe, North America, and South America). As you read about each animal, you may find that the climate (weather patterns) or the food that grows in a place affects which animals live there. On the chart, write the name of each animal, the continent on which it lives, and why it lives there.

Animal	Continent	Why It Lives There

Try not to speak with your normal voice all day long. You can use a high voice, a low voice, or a silly voice. You just cannot use your normal voice.

▶ **Write the correct symbol (<, =, >) in each box to compare the numbers.**

1. 16 ☐ 12

2. 17 ☐ 11

3. 15 ☐ 15

4. 13 ☐ 13

5. 15 ☐ 16

6. 13 ☐ 14

7. 18 ☐ 15

8. 19 ☐ 20

9. 17 ☐ 15

10. 12 ☐ 11

11. 10 ☐ 20

12. 14 ☐ 41

Make a stack of twelve books. Estimate how tall your stack is. Use a yardstick or tape measure to check your estimate.

▶ **Read each group of words. Put them in the correct order so that they form a sentence. Write the sentence on the line.**

EXAMPLE:

bought   robot   a   him   Barry's dad

Barry's dad bought him a robot.
___

1. football   The   could   play   robot

___

2. robot   Barry   Bruiser   his   named

___

3. fun   had   together   They   playing

___

Try to balance your pencil on the end of your finger so that your finger is at the middle of the pencil. Now, try to balance it straight up and down with the eraser touching your finger. Which was easier?

▶ **Follow the directions below to make the earth a better place.**

The earth is a big place. Did you know that what you do every day can affect the earth? Almost every human action does something to the earth. Think about this: If a family goes to the beach for the day and leaves behind a few soft drink cans, a newspaper, and an empty sunscreen bottle, they have had a negative effect on the earth. But, if they had simply taken the items with them and dropped them off in recycling bins, they would have had a positive effect on the earth. The metal cans, newspaper, and sunscreen bottle could be recycled and made into something new. Trash would not have littered the beach. The ocean animals would not have been hurt by the trash left behind.

Do you want to have a positive effect on the earth? Have your family members help you make a list of things you can do to be good to the earth.

_____

_____

_____

_____

_____

Use sticky notes to rate all of the foods in your kitchen by how much you like them. Use the numbers *1* through *5*. If you like the food a lot, write a *5* on the sticky note and then stick the note on the can or box. If you do not like it at all, write a *1*.

▶ **Read each story problem. Use the box next to the problem to add or subtract the numbers and solve each problem.**

Karl went surfing 38 times last summer. Steve went surfing 21 times. How many times did they go surfing altogether?

1.

Last summer, Steve lost 22 golf balls. Karl lost 20 golf balls. How many golf balls did they lose in all?

2.

Nina and Luis jog to stay fit. Nina jogs 56 miles a week. Luis jogs 32 miles a week. How many more miles does Nina jog than Luis?

3.

If you were to take a piece of paper and fold it in half, and then fold it in half again, and then fold it in half one more time, and then unfold it, how many boxes would you have made with the fold lines? Make a guess. Then, try it to check your guess.

▶ **Follow the directions below to learn more about the world outside.**

Collect several different small outdoor objects: a pinecone, a leaf, a flower, a nut, a rock, and other safe, interesting outdoor things. Put each item on the ground. Look at each item. Decide whether each item is symmetrical. *Symmetrical* means that if you cut something in half, the two sides will look the same and have the same parts. If they do, then the object is symmetrical. If they do not, then the object is asymmetrical.

Pick up a notebook and pencil. Now, take a walk. As you go, write 10 things you see. Then, write two words to describe each thing. This is good practice for writing adjectives and a great way to take a look at nature.

When you are outside, list the things you see, such as the names on your neighbors' mailboxes. Practice putting the names in ABC order. As you improve, make the list longer to include many outside objects. Challenge yourself to find something that starts with each letter of the alphabet. Good luck with *Q* and *X*!

Leave an index card inside a family book for the next person who reads the book to find. Write why you liked the book on the note card, but do not give away the ending!

▶ **Use the bar graph to answer the questions.**

Fishing Results

Number of Fish Caught	Juan	Maria	Katie	Jordan
4	■			
3	■	■		■
2	■	■	■	■
1	■	■	■	■

1. Who caught the most fish? _____

2. Who caught the fewest fish? _____

3. Who caught one fish less than Maria? _____

4. How many fish did Juan and Jordan catch altogether?

_____

5. How many fish did the children catch in all? _____

On ten index cards, write ten important things that have happened to you in your life from the time you were born until now. Mix up the cards. Give them to a family member and see if he can put them in the correct order.

Answer Key

Page 1: 1. b; 2. n; 3. b; 4. p; 5. h; 6. j

Page 2: The capital letters should be written from A to Z.

Page 3: 1. o; 2. a; 3. e; 4. u; 5. 1; 6. o

Page 4: 1. 4; 2. 2; 3. 1; 4. 8; 5. 6; 6. 10; 7. 6; 8. 6; 9. 4; 10. 8; 11. 3; 12. 7

Page 5: 1. v; 2. b; 3. f; 4. n; 5. m; 6. y

Page 6: The lowercase letters should be written from a to z.

Page 7: 1. t, n; 2. s, n; 3. c, t; 4. n, t; 5. l, p; 6. c, n

Page 8:

1. ;

2.  ; 3. 6:00;

4.  ; 5. 12:00;

6.

Page 9: 1. e; 2. i; 3. o; 4. a; 5. a; 6. i

Page 10: 1. one; 2. six; 3. three; 4. zero; 5. five; 6. ten

Page 11: 1. tape; 2. mop; 3. slide; 4. cap

Page 12: 1. 3, 4, 7, 8, 11, 12, 15, 16, 19, 20, 23, 24; 2. 32, 33, 35, 36, 38, 39, 41, 42, 44, 45, 47, 48, 50; 3. 75, 76, 79, 80, 81, 83, 84, 86, 87, 88, 90, 91, 93, 94, 96, 97, 99, 100, 101

Page 13: 1. can; 2. pan; 3. pin; 4. cube

Page 14: Students should write their first and last names.

Page 15: 1. ?; 2. .; 3. ?; 4. !; 5. .; 6. ?; 7. .; 8. ?; 9. !; 10. ?

Page 16: 1. 4; 2. 22; 3. 26; 4. 25; 5. 61

Page 17: 1. o; 2. u; 3. a; 4. e; 5. a; 6. i

Page 18: Symbols: 1. square, triangle, square, triangle; 2. star, circle, rectangle; star; 3. diamond, diamond, oval, diamond; 4. square, arrow, arrow, square; Numbers: 5. 1,2,1,2,1,2; 6. 6, 5, 4, 6, 5; 7. 9,9,8,9,9; 8. 1,5,2,5

Page 19: Students drawings will vary.

Page 20: 1. hat, bat, sat; 2. rag, tag, sag; 3. she, me, we, see; 4. rake, lake, make, bake; 5. ring, thing, wing; 6. fun, sun, spun; 7. land, sand, band

Page 21: Students drawings will vary.

Page 22: 1. 30; 2. Yes; 3. 35, 15

Page 23: 1. in–out; 2. up–down; 3. big–little; 4. tall–short; 5. new–old; 6. under–over; 7. soft–hard; 8. hot–cold; 9. off–on; 10. happy–sad; 11. go–stay; 12. yes–no

Page 24: No answer required.

Page 25: 1. 9; 2. 4; 3. 7; 4. 10

Page 26: 1. it's; 2. they've; 3. we'll; 4. I'm; 5. you'll; 6. she'll; 7. he's; 8. it'll

Page 27: 1. 4, 8, 10; 2. 16, 18, 22, 24; 3. 26, 30, 32, 36; 4. 10, 15, 25, 30; 5. 40, 50, 55, 60; 6. 70, 75, 85, 90

Page 28: 1. apple, book, cat; 2. dog, eagle, fish; 3. girl, hat, ice; 4. king, lamp, map

Page 29: 1. 24; 2. 40; 3. 33; 4. 57; 5. 26; 6. 45

Page 30: 1. bow; 2. eye; 3. sun; Drawings will vary.

302

Answer Key (continued)

Page 31: 1. 20, 30, 50, 70; 2. 40, 50, 70, 80, 90; 3. 40, 60, 70, 80, 90; 4. 30, 40, 60, 70, 80; 5. 20, 40, 50, 70; 6. 40, 60, 70, 90

Page 32: Month and dates will vary. 1. 7, 2. Answers will vary; 3. 12

Page 33: Answers will vary.

Page 34: 1. 18; 2. 13; 3. 12; 4. 17; 5. 24; 6. 37

Page 35: 1. dark; 2. girls; 3. hop; 4. wet

Page 36: 1. piano; 2. dentist; 3. store; 4. pencil; 5. teacher; 6. school; 7. nest; 8. doctor

Page 37: Answers will vary.

Page 38:

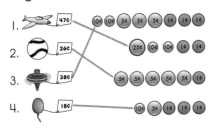

Page 39: Answers will vary.

Page 40: 1. 8; 2. 6; 3. 9; 4. 6; 5. 4; 6. 8; 7. 2; 8. 0; 9. 5

Page 41: 1. She; 2. Dr., Sharma; 3. Do, Paul, Brown; 4. We, Atlanta, December; 5. May, Sunday; 6. On, Tuesday; 7. Are, Wednesday; 8. Please, Robin, Stuart; 9. Our, Mr., Perry

Page 42: 1. 2; 2. 6

Page 43: 1. D; 2. B

Page 44: 1. ?; 2. .; 3. ?; 4. ?; 5. .; 6. .

Page 45: 1. 11; 2. 4; 3. 10; 4. 5; 5. 11; 6. 6; 7. 11; 8. 6; 9. 11; 10. 6; 11. 11; 12. 11; 13. 12; 14. 10; 15. 2

Page 46: 1. I help people get well–doctor; 2. I grow things to eat–farmer; 3. I fly airplanes–pilot; 4. I work in a school–teacher; 5. I bake cakes and bread–baker

Page 47: The following words should be colored blue: fry, tie, light, my, sigh, try, bike, sign, pie, guy, by, high, dry, bite, time, night, cry, dime, fine, lie, sight, why, right, shy, ride, buy, side, hike, kite, nine; The following words should be colored green: bib, wig, six, if, fib, gift, pit, miss, fish, lit, chin, sit, hill, hid, bill, quit, bin, mitt, tin, win, fit, will, pin, fin, zip, did

Page 48: 1. backed, baked; 2. whent, went; 3. trane, train; 4. rom, room; 5. bik, bike

Page 49: Answers will vary.

Page 50: 1. 5, 2, 3, 5; 2. 9, 2, 7, 2; 3. 8, 5 (or 3), 3 (or 5), 5 (or 3), 3 (or 5), 8, 5; 4. 7, 3 (or 4), 4 (or 3), 4, 7

Page 51: 1. white; 2. brown; 3. purple (or red); 4. blue; 5. green; 6. orange; 7. yellow; 8. black; 9. red; 10. pink

Page 52: 1. 45; 2. 31; 3. 58; 4. 40; 5. 54; 6. 63; 7. 32; 8. 80; 9. 72; 10. 60; 11. 43; 12. 31

Page 53: 1. C

Page 54: 1. 12; 2. 16; 3. 9; 4. 6; 5. 11; 6. 5; 7. 7; 8. 7; 9. 12; 10. 9; 11. 13; 12. 10

Page 55: 1. dr; 2. tr; 3. gr; 4. cl; 5. gl; 6. st

Page 56 : 1. 4; 2. 2; 3. 4; 4. 9; 5. 6; 6. 5; 7. 2; 8. 9; 9. 5; 10. 4; 11. 8; 12. 4

Page 57: 1. it's–it is; 2. we're–we are; 3. you've–you have; 4. don't–do not; 5. we'll–we will; 6. isn't–is not

Page 58:

1.

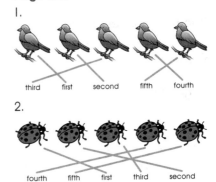

2.

Page 59: 1. Ducks like to swim; 2. Can we play in the sandbox?; 3. Some birds make nests in trees; 4. Are you having fun today?

Page 60: 1. 7; 2. 14

Answer Key (continued)

Page 61: Students should circle the cake, whale, gate, and grapes.

Page 62: 1. cookbook; 2. baseball; 3. butterfly; 4. firefighter

Page 63: Balloons 1 and 3 should be colored red. Balloons 2 and 4 should be colored blue.

Page 64: 1. 9, 9, 4, 5; 2. 2, 6, 8, 6, 2, 6; 3. 3, 7, 10, 7, 3, 10, 10, 3, 7, 10, 7, 3; 4. 1, 8, 9, 8, 1, 9, 9, 1, 8, 9, 8, 1

Page 65: 1. girl; 2. third; 3. twirl; 4. first; 5. bird; 6. circle

Page 66: 1. when; 2. who; 3. where; 4. what; 5. where; 6. when

Page 67: 1. 6; 2. 4

Page 68: Answers will vary.

Page 69: 1. C

Page 70: 1. 5+4=9; 2. 3+1=4; 3. 8+2=10

Page 71: 1. circle; 2. triangle; 3. oval; 4. pentagon

Page 72: 1. cat; 2. toys

Page 73: 1. The bee is on the flower.; 2. The bird is on the bowl.

Page 74: 1. 2; 2. 1; 3. 1; 4. 2

Page 75: 1. 30, 50, 60, 80, 90; 2. 20, 25, 30, 45, 50, 60, 65, 75, 80, 85, 95, 100; 3. 6, 10, 14, 16, 20, 24, 28, 30, 34, 36, 38, 40, 44

Page 76: 1. a; 2. o; 3. u; 4. a; 5. i; 6. i

Page 77: 1. on top of; 2. next to; 3. under

Page 78: great–a; break–a; peach–e; beat–e; leaf–e; steak–a

Page 79: 1. 4, 1; 2. 4, 5; 3. 8, 4; 4. 6, 5; 5. 7, 2; 6. 1, 7; 7. 3, 9; 8. 5, 0

Page 80: 1. last–fast; 2. bee–tree; 3. sand–band; 4. blue–glue; 5. chair–hair; 6. mean–bean; 7. main–rain

Page 81: 1. 4; 2. 2; 3. 5; 4. 3; 5. 1

Page 82: Answers will vary.

Page 83: 1. <; 2. >; 3. <; 4. >; 5. >; 6. >; 7. >; 8. <; 9. <; 10. <; 11. >; 12. >

Page 84: Color choices will vary, but the following should be colored the same color: end, finish; small, little; hear, listen; happy, glad; below, under

Page 85: 1. ant; 2. baby; 3. key; 4. dog

Page 86: No answer required.

Page 87:

1. ; 2. 4:00;

3. ; 4. 11:00;

5. ; 6. 8:30;

Page 88: 1. ch; 2. wh; 3. sh; 4. ch

Page 89: 1. 2; 2. 4

Page 90: 1. C; 2. A; 3. B

Page 91: No answer required.

Page 92: 1. big; 2. tiny; 3. loud; 4. colorful; 5. yellow; 6. fuzzy; 7. three; 8. chewy; 9. sour; 10. two

Page 93: No answer required.

Page 94: Drawings will vary.
Page 95: 2, 3, 5, 8, 9, 10, 11, 13, 14, 16, 17, 19, 20, 22, 23, 25, 27, 28, 29, 31, 32, 34, 35, 36, 38, 40, 41, 43, 44, 45, 47, 49, 50, 52, 53, 55, 56, 58, 59, 61, 62, 64, 66, 67, 68, 70, 72, 73, 75, 77, 78, 79, 81, 82, 84, 85, 86, 87, 89, 90, 92, 93, 95, 96, 98, 99

Page 96: No answer required.

Answer Key (continued)

Page 97: 1. nails; 2. boxes; 3. dishes; 4. dresses

Page 98: No answer required.

Page 99: No answer required.

Page 100: 1. 1; 2. 3; 3. 3; 4. 3

Page 101: Answers will vary.

Page 102: 1. The sun will shine today; 2. I walked a mile today (or Today I walked a mile.); 3. We painted our fence; 4. She will knit something for me.

Page 103: 1. big; 2. fast; 3. go; 4. little; 5. out; 6. slow; 7. stop; 8. up

Page 104: 1. 71; 2. 91; 3. 72; 4. 34; 5. 41; 6. 40; 7. 99; 8. 80; 9. 54; 10. 61

Page 105: 1. glue; 2. frog; 3. clock; 4. bowl

Page 106: 1. C; 2. B

Page 107: 1. hands; 2. kittens; 3. glasses; 4. inches; 5. cars; 6. clocks; 7. wishes; 8. brushes

Page 108: 1. 48¢; 2. 62¢; 3. 39¢; 4. 25¢

Page 109: No answer required.

Page 110: 1. 12; 2. 12; 3. 10; 4. 14; 5. 17; 6. 16; 7. 4; 8. 5; 9. 4; 10. 0; 11. 8; 12. 4

Page 111: 1. rake; 2. tag; 3. call; 4. gate

Page 112: 1. 4, 6; 2. 1, 9; 3. 8, 4; 4. 6, 4; 5. 40; 6. 11; 7. 93; 8. 28

Page 113: 1. horses; 2. drums; 3. boxes; 4. tables; 5. planets; 6. bears; 7. wishes; 8. shells; 9. matches; 10. bricks; 11. pumpkins; 12. glasses

Page 114: Students should draw the other half of the picture as if it were a mirror image.

Page 115: Answers will vary.

Page 116: 1. Students should draw an X on the pink circle and the green circle; 2. Students should draw an X on the light blue parallelogram; 3. Students should draw an X on the green triangle and the gold triangle; 4. Students should draw an X on the light blue trapezoid; 5. Students should draw an X on the green hexagon and the blue hexagon; 6. Students should draw an X on the gold oval.

Page 117: 1. yu, you; 2. giv, give; 3. sti, sit; 4. miks, mix; 5. ovr, over

Page 118: Answers will vary.

Page 119: Answers will vary.

Page 120: 1. Olivia lives on a farm; 2. Olivia wakes up early to do chores; 3. Answers will vary; 4. Olivia's favorite thing to do in the morning is eat breakfast.

Page 121: 1. 6; 2. 3; 3. 12; 4. 15; 5. 7; 6. 7; 7. 14; 8. 9; 9. 15; 10. 12; 11. 14; 12. 30

Page 122: No answer required.

Page 123:

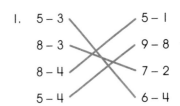

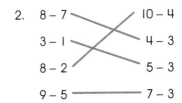

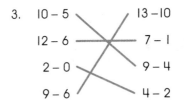

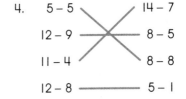

Page 124: 1. gift, his; 2. car, flat; 3. sat, the; 4. dad, store

Page 125: 1. Sidney's umbrella is old; 2. Tabby is a farm cat; 3. I think it will snow. Page 126: 1. dirty; 2. day; 3. cold; 4. dark; 5. cry

Answer Key (continued)

Page 126:

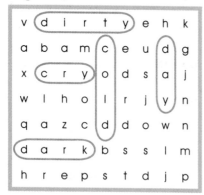

Page 127: 1. yes; 2. no; 3. yes; 4. yes

Page 128: 1. e, i, e, e, i; 2. i, e, i, e, e; 3. i, i, e, e, i

Page 129: 1. book; 2. leg; 3. cat; 4. chair; 5. apple; 6. Tom; 7. park; 8. basket

Page 130: 1. 15; 2. 12; 3. 12; 4. 15; 5. 11; 6. 16; 7. 16; 8. 11; 1. –4.; 3. –2.; 5. –8.; 7. –6

Page 131: 1. A; 2. B

Page 132: 1. 5, 6, 11, 6, 5, 11; 2. 6, 8, 14, 8, 6, 14

Page 133: 1. sang; 2. ring; 3. is; 4. ran; 5. take; 6. has

Page 134: Answers will vary.

Page 135: Possible answers: 1. Jan; 2. ban; 3. can; 4. Dan; 5. fan; 6. Nan; 7. pan; 8. ran; 9. tan; 10. van

Page 136: 1. 28¢; 2. 25; 3. 28; 4. 23

Page 137: 1. frog; 2. land; 3. stone; 4. glad; 5. most; 6. crop; 7. swim; 8. sled

Page 138: 1. 53; 2. 57; 3. 97; 4. 78; 5. 30; 6. 79

Page 139: 1. sh; 2. th; 3. ch; 4. sh

Page 140: 1. 8, 10, 12; 2. 8, 16, 20, 24; 3. 10, 20, 25

Page 141: 1. far; 2. no; 3. go; 4. tall

Page 142: 1. 14; 2. 2; 3. 5; 4. 8; 5. 20; 6. 9; 7. 1; 8. 4; 9. 7; 10. 6

Page 143: 1. eight; 2. hear; 3. sea; 4. bee; 5. wood; 6. right; 7. through; 8. knot

Page 144: Answers will vary.

Page 145: Answers will vary.

Page 146: 1. gold/fish; 2. pop/corn; 3. day/time; 4. dog/house; 5. space/ship; 6. rail/road; 7. blue/berry; 8. sail/boat; 9. grape/fruit; 10. cup/cake

Page 147: 1. 8; 2. 1; 3. 3; 4. 9; 5. 2; 6. 4; 7. 7; 8. 2; 9. 4; 10. 9; 11. 3; 12. 7; 13. 8; 14. 10; 15. 3; 16. 11

Page 148: Students should underline the following: 1. large; 2. quick; 3. happy; 4. grin; 5. bright; 6. chilly; 7. silent; Students should circle the following words: 1. little; 2. slow; 3. sad; 4. frown; 5. cloudy; 6. hot; 7. loud

Page 149: 1. 2; 2. 3; 3. 4; 4. 1; Drawings will vary.

Page 150: No answer required.

Page 151: 1. 23 should be colored blue; 2. 46 should be colored green; 3. 18 should be colored purple; 4. 54 should be colored orange; 5. 39 should be colored black; 6. 67 should be colored brown

Page 152: 1. pet; 2. barn; 3. help; 4. wet

Page 153: 1. boy, shoe; 2. she, letter, aunt; 3. you, sandwich; 4. we, movie, butterflies; 5. sister, teddy bear; 6. girl, shirt; 7. I, store, mom.

Page 154: January, February, March, April, May, June, July, August, September, October, November, December

Page 155: 1. ride; 2. swing; 3. jump; 4. swim; 5. walk; 6. run

Page 156: 1. 5, 7, 3, 9, 11; 2. 1, 7, 13, 15, 17; 3. 5, 11, 9, 13, 17, 19, 3; 4. 6, 2, 4, 8, 12; 5. 8, 10, 6, 12, 16; 6. 14, 16, 12, 18, 4, 8

Page 157: 1. m; 2. v; 3. g; 4. d; 5. m; 6. l

Page 158: 1. ?; 2. .; 3. .; 4. ?; 5. .; 6. ?; 7. .

Page 159: 1. oi; 2. ai; 3. oi; 4. oa

Answer Key (continued)

Page 160: Drawings will vary.

Page 161: 1. the American West; 2. scientists; 3. the number of ferrets increased

Page 162: 1. oy, boy; 2. oy, toy; 3. oi, soil; 4. oi, point; 5. oy, oyster; 6. oi, voice

Page 163: 1. 1, 0, 1; 2. 1, 4, 3; 3. 1, 9, 11; 4. 9, 3, 2

Page 164: 1. coin; 2. toy; 3. paw; 4. daughter; 5. boat; 6. light

Page 165: 1. can't; 2. I'm; 3. you're; 4. don't; 5. he's; 6. did not; 7. is not; 8. you have; 9. she is; 10. could not

Page 166: 1. 2, 0; 2. 1, 6; 3. 1, 4; 4. 3, 1; 5. 2, 2; 6. 1, 2; 7. 4, 7; 8. 2, 4; 9. 3, 6; 10. 5, 5; 11. 1, 1; 12. 6, 3

Page 167: 1. are; 2. is; 3. is; 4. are; 5. Is; 6. Are; Answers will vary.

Page 168: 1. ?; 2. !; 3. !; 4. ?; 5. .; 6. !; 7. .

Page 169: 1. 11; 2. 12; 3. 8; 4. 14; 5. 9; 6. 6; 7. 11; 8. 7; 9. 2; 10. 11; 11. 10; 12. 13

Page 170: 1, dog, house; 2. foot, ball; 3. fish, bowl; 4. sand, box; 5. rain, bow; 6. base, ball; 7. pan, cake; 8. fire, fighter

Page 171: 1. start; 2. close; 3. ill; 4. angry; 5. happy; 6. tidy; 7. big; 8. quick

Page 172: 1. brzea–zebra; 2. nowlf–flown; 3. owlb–bowl; 4. rpzipe–zipper; 5. leppeo–people; 6. yatdo–today; 7. oessh–shoes; 8. karp - park

Page 173: No answer required.

Page 174: 1. 10; 2. 13; 3. 13; 4. 8; 5. 11; 6. 10; 7. 12; 8. 10; 9. 10; 10. 11; 11. 7, 12. 13

Page 175: 1. finger, nail; 2. tree, house; 3. air, plane; 4. swim, suit; 5. rain, drop; 6. basket, ball; 7. sand, box; 8. fish, bowl

Page 176: 1. small; 2. automobile; 3. glad; 4. rush

Page 177: Students should circle the goat and the toe; Students should draw lines between the following: globe–<picture of globe>; notes–<picture of music notes>; boat–<picture of boat>; lines should be drawn over each o.

Page 178: Top of page: It was Joe's birthday; Bottom of page: Teena went trick-or-treating.

Page 179: 1. Students should color one section of rectangle; 2. Students should color one section of circle; 3. Students should color one section of rectangle

Page 180:

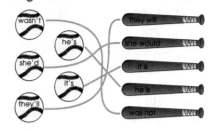

Page 181: 1. slippery, *sl* circled; 2. climb, *cl* circled; 3. play, *pl* circled; 4. flour, *fl* circled; 5–7. Answers will vary.

Page 182: 1. 78; 2. 49; 3. 39; 4. 50; 5. 15; 6. 96; 7. 28; 8. 61; 9. 88; 10. 76; 11. 41; 12. 69

Page 183: 1. bird; 2. cake; 3. bone; 4. bell; 5. bring; 6. think; 7. noon; 8. happy; 9. easy; 10. body

Page 184: 1. 52, 56, 58; 2. 60, 62, 66; 3. 68, 70, 74; 4. 75, 78, 82; 5. 86, 87, 90

Page 185: Students should circle the flute and ruler; 1. mule; 2. tune; 3. tube

Page 186: 1. oak; 2. six; 3. funny; 4. red; 5. hard; 6. furry

Page 187: 1. 14; 2. 13; 3. 11; 4. 10; 5. 16; 6. 13; 7. 18; 8. 12; 9. 11; 10. 15; 11. 12; 12. 17

Page 188: 1. hand; 2. cap; 3. lamp; Students should place an X on the following words: 4. name; 5. base; 6. snake

Answer Key (continued)

Page 189: Students should circle the following: 1. two nickels; 2. one dime, one nickel, one penny; 3. two dimes, one nickel; 4. all coins shown

Page 190: 1. ate–eight; 2. cent–sent; 3. our–hour; 4. won–one; 5. knew–new; 6. pair–pear; 7. hear–here; 8. know–no; 9. right–write; 10. blew–blue

Page 191: Student should circle the following: 1. pr; 2. br; 3. dr; 4. cr; 5. gr; 6. tr; 7. fr; 8. dr; 9. tr; 10. cr; 11. pr; 12. br; 13. dr; 14. br; 15. gr; 16. fr

Page 192: 1. 6; 2. 4; 3. 4; 4. 12; 5. 10; 6. 2; 7. 5; 8. 10; 9. 19; 10. 2; 11. 14; 12. 12; 13. 13; 14. 8; 15. 12; 16. 16

Page 193: 1. strong–weak; 2. bad–good; 3. over–under; 4. old–new; 5. happy–sad; 6. add–subtract; 7. wet–dry; 8. always–never; 9. light–dark; 10. slow–fast; 11. tall–short; 12. on–off; 13. inside–outside; 14. float–sink

Page 194: Drawing should match directions.

Page 195: Answers will vary.

Page 196: No answer required.

Page 197: 6+8–14-6; 13-4–9+4; 15-8–7+8; 8+4–12-8; 17-9–8+9

Page 198: No answer required.

Page 199: No answer required.

Page 200: 1. is; 2. is; 3. are; 4. are; 5. are; 6. is; 7. am; 8. am

Page 201: 1. 17; 2. 22; 3. 34; 4. 51; 5. 22; 6. 32; 7. 51; 8. 17

Page 202: No answered required.

Page 203: 1. 6; 2. 11; 3. 26; 4. 16; 5. 35; 6. 9

Page 204: No answer required.

Page 205: No answer required.

Page 206: 1. 18, 17, 19, 13, 14; 2. 10, 14, 12, 15, 11, 13; 3. 16, 12, 14, 13, 10, 11

Page 207: 1. can't; 2. easy; 3. key; 4. buy; 5. light; 6. once; 7. carry; 8. you're; 9. star; 10. funny

Page 208: 1. 5 + 8 = 13, 13 - 8 = 5, 13 - 5 = 8; 2. 5 + 7 = 12, 7 + 5 = 12, 12 - 7 = 5, 12 - 5 = 7; 3. 8 + 6 = 14, 6 + 8 = 14, 14 - 6 = 8, 14 - 8 = 6

Page 209: Student should write the following words under *nose*: coat, drove, rope, those; Students should write the following words under *pop*: fox, job, rock, top

Page 210: 1. 0, 2, 5, 6, 3; 2. 7, 6, 4, 5, 3, 8; 3. 9, 5, 7, 3, 6, 4

Page 211: 1. ir; 2. or; 3. ar; 4. ur; 5. or; 6. ar

Page 212: 1. 9 miles; 2. 9 miles

Page 213: 1. no; 2. no; 3. yes; 4. no; 5. yes; 6. no; 7. no

Page 214: 1. 36; 2. 39; 3. 58; 4. 69; 5. 99; 6. 39; 7. 95; 8. 80; 9. 49; 10. 79; 11. 99; 12. 59

Page 215: 1. j; 2. j; 3. g; 4. g; 5. g; 6. j; 7. j; 8. j; 9. g

Page 216: 1. 0 hundreds, 4 tens, 8 ones = 48; 2. 1 hundred, 4 tens, 4 ones = 144; 3. 1 hundred, 1 ten, 5 ones = 115; 4. 1 hundred, 3 tens, 7 ones = 137

Page 217: 1–2. Answers will vary.

Page 218: Students should circle the following: 1. snowman; 2. shirt; 3. spider; Students should write the following: 4. stamp; 5. twins; 6. snow; 7. sky

Page 219: 1. 96; 2. 21; 3. 82; 4. 37; 5. 65; 6. 61; 7. 79; 8. 58; 9. 22; 10. 80; 11. 18; 12. 100; 13. 12; 14. 20; 15. 44; 16. 34

Page 220: 1. F; 2. G; 3. E; 4. B; 5. A; 6. J; 7. D; 8. I; 9. H; 10. C

Page 221: 1. 2; 2. 3; 3. 5

Page 222: 1. was; 2. was; 3. was; 4. was; 5. were; 6. were; 7. were; 8. was; 9. were

Page 223: 1. A lost cat; 2. The cat is big, has spots, and runs fast.

Answer Key (continued)

Page 224: Students should color the following: 1. 23; 2. 57; 3. 52; 4. 26; 5. 39; 6. 10

Page 225: Student should write the following words under *cow*: brown, clown, crown, how, tower; Students should write the following words under *pillow*: blow, bowl, elbow, mow, own

Page 226: 1. A.; 2. E; 3. F; 4. C; 5. B; 6. D

Page 227: 1. 67¢; 2 . 68¢; 3. 67¢; 4. 75

Page 228: Answers will vary.

Page 229 1. +2; 2. –2; 3. +10; 4. –1

Page 230: 1. ck; 2. gr; 3. sh; 4. sh; 5. sl; 6. ng

Page 231: 1. A; 2. a person who collects stamps for a hobby

Page 232: 1. 1/4; 2. 2/3; 3. 1/2

Page 233: 1. fireworks; 2. grandfather; 3. cartwheel; 4. sunflower; 5. snowflakes; 6. waterfall

Page 234: 1. duck; 2. fly; 3. roar; 4. hop; 5. bark; 6. bird

Page 235: 1. 11, 10, 15, 17 (circled); 2. 16, 9, 18 (circled), 12; 3. 9, 10, 13, 16 (circled); 4. 11, 4, 14 (circled), 13

Page 236: B, C

Page 237: 1. 11 cm; 2. 9 cm

Page 238: No answer required.

Page 239: 1. dark; 2. wet; 3. girls; 4. hop; 5. train

Page 240: 1. washing the car; 2. bundling newspapers; 3. $7.00; 4. $ .50

Page 241: 1. N; 2. Y; 3. Y; 4. N; 5. Y; 6. N; 7. Y; 8. N

Page 242: 1. Students should color three sections of rectangle; 2. Students should color one part of circle; 3. Students should color one part of rectangle; 4. Students should color two parts of circle

Page 243: Student should write the following words under *celery*: center, cereal, circle, city, cent; Students should write the following words under *cat*: cake, camp, candy, coat, corn

Page 244: 1. 55 students; 2. 91 shells; 3. 32 laps; 4. 84 fish

Page 245: 1–3. Answers will vary.

Page 246: 1. 6 + 7 = 13, 7 + 6 = 13, 13 - 7 = 6, 13 - 6 = 7; 2. 7 + 8 = 15, 8 + 7 = 15, 15 - 7 = 8, 15 - 8 = 7; 3. 6 + 8 = 14, 8 + 6 = 14, 14 - 8 = 6, 14 - 6 = 8; 4. 7 + 5 = 12, 5 + 7 = 12, 12 - 7 = 5, 12 - 5 = 7

Page 247: Answers will vary.

Page 248: 1. 21; 2. 3; 3. 16; 4. 6

Page 249: 1. cat–hat; 2. but–rut; 3. pig–big; 4. hen–ten; 5. log–fog; 6. cake–rake; 7. rice–mice; 8. sheep–jeep; 9. bone–cone; 10. chute–flute

Page 250: Answers will vary.

Page 251: 1. sight–storm clouds moving in; 2. touch–tiny sprinkles on my face; 3. taste–little drops inside my mouth; 4. hearing–tapping a rhythm on the window; 5. smell–clean, fresh air

Page 252: 1. 1, 2; 2. 9, 3; 3. 4, 4; 4. 7, 6; 5. 8, 1; 6. 5, 5; 7. 3, 9; 8. 6, 0

Page 253: 1. table; 2. square; 3. sky; 4. light

Page 254: 1. 12:00; 2. 9:15; 3. 2:30; 4. 4:00

Page 255: 1. a, part, ment; 2. e, nor, mous; 3. sub, trac, tion; 4. won, der, ful; 5. ad, ven, ture

Page 256: 1. 500; 2. 900; 3. 300; 4. 1,000; 5. 800; 6. 700; 7. 600; 8. 900

Page 257: 1. 1, 3; 2. 4, 35; 3. 6, 57; 4. 5, 49; 5. 3, 21

Page 258:

Kate	X	X	X	O
Grace	X	O	X	X
Jade	O	X	X	X
Meghan	X	X	O	X

Answer Key (continued)

Page 259: Answers will vary.

Page 260: I. F; 2. F; 3. T; 4. T; 5. walk, 6. go; 7. tired; 8. full

Page 261: I. 600; 2. 300; 3. 100; 4. 200; 5. 500; 6. 500; 7. 0

Page 262: No answer required.

Page 263: I. place; 2. place; 3. person; 4. thing; 5. thing; 6. person; 7. person; 8. thing

Page 264: I. 10, 12, 14, 16, 18, 20, Rule: +2; 2. 40, 50, 60, 70, 80, 90, Rule: +10; 3. 20, 25, 30, 35, 40, 45, Rule: +5; 4. 15, 18, 21, 24, 27, 30, Rule: +3

Page 265: Answers will vary.

Page 266: I. 9; 2. 6; 3. 12; 4. 15; 5. 12; 6. 8; 7. 20; 8. 16

Page 267: Student should write the following words under *Nouns for People*: aunt, cousin, dad, girl; Students should write the following words under *Nouns for Places*: basement, restaurant, bedroom, France; Student should list the following words under *Nouns for Things*: lamp, dresser, chair, sink

Page 268: I. 3, 4, 1, 300, 40, 1; 2. 5, 6, 3, 500, 60, 3; 3. 7, 5, 2, 700, 50, 2; 4. 8, 4, 5, 800, 40, 5; 5. 4, 2, 9, 400, 20, 9; 6. 6, 8, 4, 600, 80, 4

Page 269: I. a; 2. a; 3. a; 4. an; 5. an; 6. a; 7. a; 8. a; 9. an; 10. an; II. a; 12. an; 13. a; 14. an

Page 270: I. B; 2. A tiny seedling begins to grow.

Page 271: I–2. Answers will vary.

Page 272: I. six; 2. hairy; 3. hard; 4. black; 5. beautiful; 6. powerful; 7. four; 8. green

Page 273: I. The most common pets are cats and dogs; 2. A pet needs food, exercise, and a good place to live; 3. The best thing you can give your pet is love.

Page 274: No answer required.

Page 275: I. 4; 2. 9; 3. 9; 4. 9; 5. 6; 6. 9; 7. 4; 8. 8; 9. 9; 10. 4; II. 6; 12. 9

Page 276: I. O; 2. F; 3. F; 4. O; 5. O; 6. F

Page 277: I. C; 2. Its position as viewed from Earth changes throughout the month.; 3. when Earth is between the sun and the moon

Page 278: I. Students should circle 7-5 and 5-3; 2. Students should circle 9-8 and 4-3; 3. Students should circle 7-2 and 5-0; 4. Students should circle 6-6 and 9-9.

Page 279: I. O; 2. F; 3. F; 4. O

Page 280: I–6. Answers will vary.

Page 281: I. B; 2. They are important for chewing food; 3. They fall out and are replaced by adult teeth; 4. 32

Page 282: I. 23; 2. 20; 3. 25; 4. 59; 5. 28; 6. 63; 7. 27; 8. 63; 9. 67; 10. 26; II. 29; 12. 17

Page 283: I. two; 2. too; 3. to; 4. too; 5. to; 6. to; 7. to; 8. two

Page 284: I. 3 inches; 2. 10 inches; 3. ninth; 4. II inches

Page 285: I. noun; 2. verb; 3. noun; 4. noun; 5. noun; 6. noun; 7. noun; 8. verb; 9. verb; 10. noun

Page 286: Students should circle the following items: I, 2, 5, 7, 8, 10, II, 12

Page 287: I. verb; 2. noun; 3. adjective; 4. noun; 5. noun; 6. verb; 7. noun; 8. adjective

Page 288: No answer required.

Page 289: I. can; 2. have; 3. are; 4. is; 5. was (underlined), calling (circled); 6. am (underlined), going (circled); 7. are (underlined), playing (circled); 8. were (underlined), running (circled); 9. might (underlined), go (circled); 10. could (underlined), eat (circled)

Answer Key (continued)

Page 290: 1. twenty-three–23, seventy-five–75, sixty-two–62, ninety-nine–99, eighteen–18, thirty-two–32, eleven–11; 2. fifteen–15, eighty-four–84, forty-seven–47, twenty-six–26, fifty-three–53, twelve–12, one hundred–100

Page 291: No answer required.

Page 292: No answer required.

Page 293: 1. Missy and Kim; 2. winter; 3. bark of a tree; 4. the woods; 5. It was too cold.

Page 294: Answers will vary.

Page 295: 1. >; 2. >; 3. =; 4. =; 5. <; 6. <; 7. >; 8. <; 9. >; 10. >; 11. <; 12. <

Page 296: 1. The robot could play football; 2. Barry named his robot Bruiser; 3. They had fun playing together.

Page 297: Answers will vary.

Page 298: 1. 38 + 21 = 59; 2. 22 + 20 = 42; 3. 56 - 32 = 24

Page 299: No answer required.

Page 300: 1. Juan; 2. Katie; 3. Katie; 4. 7; 5. 12

Summer Quest™

Summer Workbook Series

Congratulations!

This certifies that

_____

Name

has completed **Summer Quest**™ Activities.

_____

Parent's Signature